THE SPIRIT-FILLED LIFE

Be filled with the Spirit. – Ephesians 5:18

THE SPIRIT-FILLED LIFE

RESTORING A BIBLICAL UNDERSTANDING AND EXPERIENCE OF THE HOLY SPIRIT

John MacNeil, B. A.

We love hearing from our readers. Please contact us at www.anekopress.com/questions-comments with any questions, comments, or suggestions.

Printed in the United States of America
Aneko Press

www.anekopress.com

Aneko Press, Life Sentence Publishing, and our logos are trademarks of
Life Sentence Publishing, Inc.
203 E. Birch Street
P.O. Box 652
Abbotsford, WI 54405

RELIGION / Christian Theology / Pneumatology

Paperback ISBN: 978-1-62245-541-6
eBook ISBN: 978-1-62245-542-3

10 9 8 7 6 5 4 3 2

Available where books are sold

Contents

Register This New Book

Benefits of Registering*

- ✓ FREE **replacements** of lost or damaged books

- ✓ FREE **audiobook** – *Pilgrim's Progress,* audiobook edition

- ✓ FREE information about new titles and other **freebies**

Editor's Foreword

Since John MacNeil first wrote *The Spirit-Filled Life* in 1894, much has changed in our world. Yet the truth found in the Word of God is timeless. This makes the heart of MacNeil's message timeless as well.

We have edited this modern adaptation in order to add clarity to the language and expressions MacNeil used over a century ago, meaning this book has been significantly edited from the original. Chapter divisions have been modified, and we added subheadings. Yet in the process, we've been careful to stay true to the heart of the message and to MacNeil's unique writing voice. We have researched terms to provide an appropriate substitute from today's vocabulary. Our goal is to bring a new audience of readers to appreciate the timeless message about the importance of being filled with the Holy Spirit.

Added reference information and biographical notes

provide a starting point if readers wish to complement their reading with additional research.

The Scriptures used throughout the book have been updated to the *New American Standard Bible*, except for as noted where the author used a phrase that was specific to another translation.

We hope to provide a new understanding of what it means to be filled with the Holy Spirit – a life-changing experience that transcends any barriers of time and applies to readers of yesterday and today.

Introduction
by Andrew Murray and
H. B. Macartney Jr.

I have been asked to write a few lines introducing this book to American Christians. I count it a privilege to be allowed to do so.

The one thing needful for the church of Christ in our day and for every member of it, is to be filled with the spirit of Christ. Christianity is nothing except for being a ministry of the Spirit. Preaching is nothing except for being a demonstration of the Spirit. Holiness is nothing except for being the fruit of the Spirit. These truths are so seldom taught or emphasized as they should be, and the blessings they speak of are so seldom experienced, that one gladly welcomes every voice that draws attention to them.

We know that all do not perfectly agree on the best answer to the question: How can we be filled with the

Spirit? Some press the aspect of truth that reminds us the Holy Spirit *has been given* to the church and that he dwells in every believer, a fountain of living water. In the same way as there have been fountains clogged by stones and earth that only need to be cleared and opened up, so we only need to remove the hindrances, to yield ourselves in perfect surrender to the Spirit in us, and the filling will come. We must not ask God for more of the Spirit. God asks for more of us so that the Spirit may wholly have us.

Others, while fully admitting that the Spirit is in the believer and that the Spirit asks for a more entire surrender, will still urge that we must ask for and receive the filling of the Spirit directly from God. God cannot give his spiritual gifts apart from himself, once for all. As the Divine and everlasting One, he gives unceasingly. The Spirit has not been given as if he had left heaven. He is in God and in the church. It is from God himself that larger measures of the Spirit must always be sought and received.

Among those who hold this latter view, there is again some diversity in the representation of truth. On the one hand, we are reminded that it is *by faith* we receive the Holy Spirit and that faith often has to rest and to act without any conscious experience – it has to walk in the dark. Souls that are fully surrendered to God are invited to claim the promise and then to go and work in the full assurance that the Spirit is in them and will work through them in his fullness. On the other hand, some stress the words *we receive the Spirit* by faith. The difference between believing and receiving is pointed out, and we are urged to wait until we receive what we claim and know that God has filled us with his Spirit again. "To be filled with the Spirit" is offered us as a definite, conscious experience.

With still other Christians, we find what may be regarded as a combination of these different views. They believe some have received a very definite, conscious filling of the Spirit and this may be had by all. Though from their own experience they cannot testify of it; they still look for God to do for them above what they have asked or thought. Meanwhile, they know God's Spirit is in them and they seek grace to know him better, and they seek to yield themselves to him more undividedly. They believe the Spirit within them is himself leading them on to the Lord above them, whose role it is to fill with the Spirit. In faith they have claimed the fullness. They have placed themselves to be filled; they look to their Lord to fulfill his promise. Whether it comes in one swift moment or more gradually, they know it is theirs.

I have written this with an eye to those who may not entirely agree with the way in which the truth is presented in this little book. I wish to urge all, especially ministers of the gospel, to give it a prayerful reading. I feel confident it will bring them help and blessing. It will deepen the conviction of the great need and absolute duty of being filled with the Spirit. It will point out the hindrances and open up the way. It will stir up faith and hope. And I trust it will bring many people to feel that it is at the footstool of the throne – in the absolute surrender of a new consecration – that the blessing is to be received from God himself.

May this book stir up all its readers, not only to seek this blessing for themselves, but also to cry earnestly, *keep praying most earnestly* (1 Thessalonians 3:10) *for all the saints* (Ephesians 6:18), that God may give the Holy Spirit in power throughout his whole church. It is when the tide comes in that every pool is filled and all the separate little pools are lost in the great ocean. As all believers who know or seek this blessing begin to pray as intensely for each other and all their brethren as for themselves, this is when the power of the Spirit will be fully known. With the prayer that this Spirit-filled book may be greatly blessed of God, I commend it to the study of his children.

Andrew Murray

Introduction to the American edition, December 1895

* * *

Christian reader, I pray that before you finish this little book you may become so eager, so intense in your longings after God, that you will not be satisfied until you are really and actually "full" of him and filled with the Holy Spirit.

When the Lord asked Job, *Can you lift up your voice to the clouds, So that an abundance of water will cover you?* (Job 38:34), he would undoubtedly have answered no.

On the other hand, with all humility but without the slightest hesitation, we can answer yes. Abundance is the Father's will; the provisions of life in Jesus are abundant. The stream of the Spirit's energies is abounding forever and ever.

> *And God is able to make all grace abound*
> *to you, so that always having all sufficiency*
> *in everything, you may have an abundance*
> *for every good deed.* (2 Corinthians 9:8)

We only need to reflect a little until the truth flashes, and then the victory is all but won. We only need to consider who it was that first loved us and called us to be his own children when we were wandering in sin's desert. Who was it that first crossed the wild with a cup of living water to quench our dying thirst? Who now crosses that desert a second time on our behalf with great camel-loads of wine and milk? What did it cost him to draw that water from salvation's well, or to buy those luxuries for growth and power? What will one healing, stimulating swallow accomplish in us and others? How will he grieve if we decline to "buy," or hesitate to "drink"?

> *Ho! Every one who thirsts, come to the waters;*
> *And you who have no money come, buy*
> *and eat. Come, buy wine and milk Without*
> *money and without cost.* (Isaiah 55:1)

Above all, what will be the consequences to his glory? Oh, let's arise! Let's *shake* ourselves *from the dust* (Isaiah 52:2). Let's drink abundantly, beloved! There is just now an unutterable need for something more. Single souls are drooping, though divinely planted. Churches are full of bones, very many and very dry.[1] The world is a jungle, a forest ready for the fire. Men, women, and children form one vast continent of feeling, of ever-increasing sensibility, with an ever-deepening and ever-aching void. Even the teachers of high truth themselves are not *filled of the abundance of Your house,*

---

1   See Ezekiel 37; Lamentations 4:8; Psalm 102:3.

and they do not *drink* deep enough *of the river of Your delights* (Psalm 36:8).

Yes, there is a thirst not quenched, and I am persuaded that we can only quench Immanuel's thirst when, in him, we quench our own. Then let's make haste to God; let's hurry to the stream that is full of water. We cannot know what the infilling of the Spirit means until we are in-filled. It is a new experience. God is not thereby better seen than before by nature's eye, but he is better understood, better loved, better leaned on; that is what he wants, and that is enough.

Perhaps, dear reader, the pathway between you and blessing is somewhat hidden, or your eyes are dim, or your heart is only beating with a faint desire. If so, then carefully read this little book; read it beside an open Bible; read it in prayer. Through infinite compassion, it may prove to be a key into the place of abundance (Psalm 66:12). It may tear the veil, scatter the darkness, lead you to joy unspeakable!

I have known the author long and love him much. He is thoroughly trained in theology, and he is a first-rate preacher. He presents the gospel for sinners as clear as crystal, and when you have read a little further, you will say the same of his gospel for saints! He has penetrated far into *the shelter of the Most High* (Psalm 91:1) and so can speak from a rich experience of his own, to which, however, he never refers.

I cannot but express the hope that this little treatise on the Spirit-filled life may not only be widely circulated in Australia, but also in England and America. It is fresh, it is simple, it is temperate, it is timely, it is scriptural, and it is splendid. It sets forth a promise to be claimed, a gift to be received, a command to be obeyed, and it portrays the sequel – more liberty, more peace, more devotion, more fellowship with the Son of God in his rejection by man, in his fellowship with the Father.

H. B. Macartney Jr.

Introduction to the Australian edition, July 1894

Author's Preface

I have written only for the spiritual babes. I ask the full-grown – the "perfect" or complete – who may read this to kindly bear this in mind. A wide and more or less intimate acquaintance with the churches of Australasia has shown me the need for a simple, familiar talk, such as this little book professes to be. Many – oh, so many – of God's dear children are living on the wrong side of Pentecost, living on the same plane as that on which the disciples were living before they were filled with the Holy Spirit, and thus by their lives they practically make the sad confession, "We did not so much as hear whether the Holy Spirit was given or whether there is any Holy Spirit."

> It happened that while Apollos was at
> Corinth, Paul passed through the upper
> country and came to Ephesus, and found

> *some disciples. He said to them, "Did you*
> *receive the Holy Spirit when you believed?"*
> *And they said to him, "No, we have not*
> *even heard whether there is a Holy Spirit.*
> (Acts 19:1-2)

The object of this little work is to call their attention to their birthright, to the fact that the fullness of the Spirit is the birthright of every believer. God wants us to live on *this* side of Pentecost, not the *other* side.

The substance of the following pages has been occasionally delivered as a series of afternoon Bible readings in connection with my mission services. I have been persuaded to commit them to writing because of frequent requests from those who heard them and want to have them in a more permanent form, along with the hope that the great blessing that has most graciously been given to them when spoken might not be withheld from them when being read.

I gratefully acknowledge help received from many sources, both in preparing the Bible readings and in preparing them for publication. I especially owe a debt of gratitude to my beloved *helper in Christ,*[2] who has now for many years been *a helper of many and of myself also,*[3] the Rev. H. B. Macartney, M. A. He has

---

2   Romans 16:9
3   Romans 16:2

most kindly revised my manuscript, penned an introduction, and encouraged me to publish.

In *fear and in much trembling*[4] because of its inadequateness, but with earnest and unceasing prayer to the One who has been pleased before today to use *the weak things of the world to shame the things which are strong* (1 Corinthians 1:27) – with the prayer asking him to graciously do so again – I send this little messenger forth on its mission, trusting that the reading of it may be as great a blessing to every reader as the writing of it has been to the writer.

Suggestions for How to Use This Book

- Peruse it for personal pleasure and benefit.

- Read it aloud to the young folks.

- Use it for reading lessons with children or foreigners seeking a better knowledge of English.

- Present it to someone you meet out and about or to someone calling at your door.

- Keep it and other books circulating as a library.

---

4   1 Corinthians 2:3

- Offer it and others as rewards to Sunday school scholars for punctuality, regular attendance, or for the memorizing of Scripture, etc.

- Forward it to a work camp or prison, to sailors, soldiers, firemen, and other neglected classes.

- Leave it and others in barber shops, waiting rooms, offices, railroad stations, etc.

- Make a list of friends or acquaintances who should read the book; send the book to the first named, ask him to pass it on to the second, and so on.

- Suggest to someone the thought of doing "book-missionary" work with it and other volumes of the same series.

- Show it to a friend; tell him how good it is and how inexpensive to circulate.

- Call the attention of your local bookseller to it, and urge them to carry a line of the books from the same publisher.

Chapter 1

The Starting Point

Reader, are you a B. A.? This little book is only for those who possess that degree from the King's College. If you are not "Born Again," please put it aside, for this is our starting point in considering the fullness of the Spirit as the birthright of every believer. If you have not been born again you have no right by birth to this, the highest of New Testament blessings. Your first concern is to become one of the children of God, and then you may inquire about your inheritance. If you *are* born again, ask that you may read with an anointed eye and with an unprejudiced mind, for the amount of prejudice that exists against this subject is extremely saddening.

In nothing that he ever wrote does John Bunyan's masterful genius appear more clearly than when, in *The Holy War*, he places that mean-spirited old Mr.

Prejudice – with sixty deaf men under him – as warden of Ear-gate. Nothing that even Emmanuel may say can reach Mansoul while Prejudice and his deaf men keep that gate.

* * *

"There is nothing about this in the standards of our church."

"I have not met with this truth in my favorite authors."

"It is quite new to me, and I never will believe it."

And so on.

These and similar others are illustrations we might encounter that demonstrate how well Prejudice keeps his word! In the name of the Lord, let's dislodge him and determine to give a fair hearing to whatever of God's truth is presented in the following pages, no favor being asked for. Deep-rooted prejudice is one of the causes of the appalling spiritual poverty that abounds – yes, appalling when we consider the treasures within our reach.

Chapter 2

Every Believer's Birthright

All around God's people feel and express a lack of something. Their Christian experience is not what they expected it would be. Instead of expected victory, it is often recurring, dreaded defeat. Instead of soul satisfaction, it is soul hunger; instead of deep, abiding heart rest, it is disquiet and discontent; instead of advancing, it is losing ground. Is this all Christ meant when he said, *Come to Me* in Matthew 11:28? Is this life of constant disappointment the normal life of the Bible Christian? To these sad questionings the divine Word answers with an emphatic "No!" And the testimony of an ever-increasing number of God's children answers no, as well.

For this widely felt, though sometimes inarticulate demand, the divine supply is the fullness of the Spirit; this fullness is the birthright of *every* believer, a birthright by virtue of their new birth. Sometimes we hear it said that to be filled with the Spirit is the Christian privilege, but *birthright* is a stronger word.

Reader, it is your birthright to be filled with the Spirit as Peter was filled, as Stephen was filled, as the 120 men and women in the upper room were filled (Acts 2:4; 1:14-15), and as the men and women in Cornelius's house were filled (Acts 10:44-47).

> *Peter said to them, "Repent, and each of*
> *you be baptized in the name of Jesus Christ*
> *for the forgiveness of your sins; and you will*
> *receive the gift of the Holy Spirit. "For the*
> *promise is for you and your children and for*
> *all who are far off, as many as the Lord our*
> *God will call to Himself." (Acts 2:38-39)*

What have you done with your birthright? Have you claimed it? Are you living at this moment in the possession and enjoyment of it? Or are you Esau-like and despise your birthright (Genesis 25:34)? Or if you don't despise it, have you neglected it? Esau's eyes were ultimately opened to his mistake in parting with his birthright for *a single meal*, and he then desired to inherit the blessing, seeking it *with tears*, but unfortunately, his awakening came too late (Hebrews 12:16-17). I hope every reader of these lines will have the desire graciously awakened – if it has not yet been awakened and satisfied – to inherit their birthright blessing while repentance can be found. May the prediction be fulfilled in our glad experience:

> *But on Mount Zion there will be those who escape, And it will be holy. And the house of Jacob will possess their possessions.*
> (Obadiah 1:17)

Chapter 3

A Command to Be Obeyed

There may be some who would think, "It is optional for me whether I claim my birthright or not. No doubt, it would be a very fitting thing for some people to be filled with the Spirit, but *I* do not need to worry about it." In case anyone would be tempted to speak and act like this, let's understand that *be filled with the Spirit* (Ephesians 5:18) is a command to be obeyed, a duty to be done.

> *And do not get drunk with wine, for that*
> *is dissipation, but be filled with the Spirit,*
> *speaking to one another in psalms and*
> *hymns and spiritual songs, singing and*
> *making melody with your heart to the Lord;*
> *always giving thanks for all things in the*
> *name of our Lord Jesus Christ to God, even*

*the Father; and be subject to one another in
the fear of Christ.* (Ephesians 5:18-21)

Many of God's people acknowledge that they did not
know that *be filled with the Spirit* was a command; but
it is, and there is no excuse for not knowing. You will
notice that in Ephesians 5:18 there is a double command: a negative, *do not get drunk*, and a positive, *be
filled*. The positive command is as authoritative as the
negative, and was binding on just as many of those
Ephesian Christians as was the negative command.

Now what was true for those believers there in
Ephesus long ago is equally true for all believers on
God's footstool today. Is it a sin for a believer today to
disobey the command, *do not get drunk*? And is it then
a virtue to disobey the equally authoritative command,
be filled? If it is a sin for a Christian to be drunk, it is
just as surely, truly, and really a sin not to be filled.
We are commanded and expected to live a Spirit-filled
life, to be filled not with wine – the fruit of the vines
of earth – but with the new wine of the kingdom, the
fruit of the "true Vine."

Reader, imagine you are asked, "Do you obey the
command to *not get drunk with wine*?" What is your
answer? If it is yes, that is obedience. Now you are
asked, "Do you obey the command to *be filled with
the Spirit*?" What is your answer? If it is no, that is

disobedience; you are guilty of breaking one of God's simplest commandments. You have no more license to break this command than you have to break any command in the Decalogue – all ten commandments. Before you read further, shouldn't you confess your sin and tell the Master that you decide in your heart to have new obedience?

Chapter 4

Something Different
from the New Birth

B eing filled with the Spirit is a definite blessing, which is quite distinct from being born of the Spirit. Some people object that every Christian has the Spirit; quite true, for *you are not in the flesh but in the Spirit, if indeed the Spirit of God dwells in you. But if anyone does not have the Spirit of Christ, he does not belong to Him* (Romans 8:9). Also, *no one can say, "Jesus is Lord," except by the Holy Spirit* (1 Corinthians 12:3). But to have the Spirit and to be filled with the Spirit are two different things.

"Egypt always has the Nile," as someone has said, "but Egypt waits every year for its overflow." Having the Nile is one thing, but having the Nile overflowing is quite another. Now it is the Nile's overflow that is Egypt's salvation, and to overflow it must first be filled.

In the same way, it is through the Christian's overflow that the Gospel is shared with the lost, and in order to overflow there must first be the filling.

As far as God is concerned, there is no reason why this filling should not take place at the hour of conversion, of the new birth. See the case of Cornelius and his friends in Acts 10:44-48. They believed, were saved, received the Holy Spirit, and were baptized with water the same day. But it would be a fatal blunder to assert that *all* people receive the Holy Spirit in a similar manner at the moment of believing, or that they were thus filled with the Spirit. Most certainly in Bible times it was not so.

The Apostles

Consider the case of the apostles themselves. In Acts 2:4 we read, *And they were all filled with the Holy Spirit and began to speak with other tongues, as the Spirit was giving them utterance*, all in the upper room, men and women, including the twelve apostles. Now, these men had the Spirit before. When Christ called them to follow him – when they were converted – they received the Spirit. After his resurrection, but before his ascension, Christ breathed on them and said, *"Receive the Holy Spirit"* (John 20:22), and of course they did receive the Spirit then. But it is never said of them that they were filled with the Holy Spirit until that morning in the upper room, for the simple reason that it could not be said of them, *for the Spirit was not yet given* (John 7:39). Yet these men were Christians before that morning.

The Samaritans

Consider the Samaritans. In Acts 8:5-13 we find that under the preaching of Philip the evangelist, there was a work of grace in the city of Samaria, and the people believed and were baptized. These people, then, were Christians, but they were not filled with the Spirit until Peter and John came down and prayed for them, thus perfecting the work Philip had been doing (Acts 8:15-17).

Paul the Apostle

Saul was converted when the omnipotent, omnipresent Christ, standing as a picket guard (a guard of horse and foot, always ready in case of alarm) for a little church at Damascus, unhorsed him, and took him prisoner on the Damascus road. *Lord, what wilt thou have me to do?* (Acts 9:6 JUB). That question sounds like conversion, surely. For three days he lay in darkness in Damascus, a surrendered, believing man, and therefore a Christian man, but it was not until Ananias came to him that he was filled with the Holy Spirit (Acts 9:17).

Who was this Ananias, through whom even Saul – destined to prove himself the truest, bravest, grandest servant the Lord Jesus ever had – received the greatest of the New Testament blessings? Ananias was an obscure, obedient believer of whom we know nothing other than that he did this service for Saul.

Here is the ministry of the saints. So it may be today, some big Paul may be blessed through the ministry of some little Ananias.

The Ephesians

In Acts 19:1-6 Paul met some Ephesian believers – twelve men who were disciples and had been believers for some time when Paul found them. In other words, they were saved, and they were Christians. But Paul's first question to them was, *"Did you receive the Holy Spirit when you believed?"* This plainly showed that Paul thought it was possible for them to have been believers and to not yet have received the Holy Spirit. Indeed, in this case, what Paul considered a possibility turned out to be a fact; they had not yet received the Spirit.

Of course, in a certain sense, they had the Spirit; it was by the Spirit they had believed, and if they did not have the Spirit of Christ, they were not his. But for all that, they had not yet received the Spirit in the

Pentecostal sense of the word, in the sense in which Paul meant it. They had not yet come to *their* Pentecost.

Paul asked, *"Did you receive the Holy Spirit when you believed?"* This proves first that it is possible to receive the Holy Spirit at the moment of believing, and second that it is possible to believe without receiving.

After Paul had instructed them more fully in the Word and way of the Lord, we read that *the Holy Spirit came on them* (Acts 19:6). From this we conclude that these men of Ephesus obtained a blessing subsequent to their conversion, spoken of here as receiving the Holy Spirit, as the Holy Spirit "coming" on them.

This is in strict accord with what Paul himself says of this event when writing to the Ephesians: *Having also believed, you were sealed in Him with the Holy Spirit of promise* (Ephesians 1:13). First, they believed, and then, at some time after believing, they were "sealed," they received, and they were filled. From these four cases – the apostles, the Samaritans, Saul, and the Ephesians – we conclude that in New Testament times people actually lived as Christians, were saved, converted people, and yet knew nothing of the filling with the Spirit. This knowledge, this blessing, came to them some time after they were born again. Yet this is the very thing some people deny today!

Who are we to believe? These objectors or the sacred record? The divine Word declares it, and there is then no room or need for argument. So we affirm that it is equally possible for believers – for saved, converted people – to live in our own time, as well as in Bible times, without the fullness; even more, it is possible for them to live for years, then die and go home to heaven to be there forever with the Lord, and to have known nothing on earth of what it was to be filled with the Spirit. But what a loss they have suffered! Eternal, irreparable loss!

So we conclude it is abundantly plain from Scripture that for the regenerate soul there is in Christ another blessing over and above the being born of the Spirit, which is spoken of as "the fullness of the Spirit."

"I am amazed at a man like you going to these conventions," a man once said to his minister. "What new thing can these convention speakers tell you? It is all in the New Testament."

"Yes," he replied, "that's the trouble, and we have left these things in the New Testament, whereas we want to get them out of the New Testament and into our hearts and lives."

In Jesus Christ, God's Treasury, our share of Pentecost's blessing has been deposited for each of us by our Father God. Have we claimed and received our share? Not likely, if we are not aware that there *is* such a blessing for us. But once we recognize it is there, we surely will not rest until we have made it our own. The

Scottish bankers have published the fact that they have a sum of £40,000,000 (approximately $50 million[5]) – in unclaimed deposits lying in their vaults. Some of those who owned a share of this money may have died in the workhouse; some of them may be living to this moment in direst need, and they might have their money for the claiming, but they do not know that it is theirs. What vast unclaimed deposits are lying in God's Treasury, Christ! Some of his people have died spiritually poor; some are living today in spiritual poverty, a hand-to-mouth existence, with such *unfathomable riches of Christ* (Ephesians 3:8) lying "at call," at deposit in their name.

What have we done with our deposit? We are responsible for its use and disuse. Remember, the reckoning day is coming (Matthew 25:19).

---

5   With inflation, equaling about $1,522,823,028.00 today.

Chapter 5

Everybody's Need

S ome people have the idea that this blessing of the fullness of the Spirit is only for a favored few, for those who have some special work to do for God, but not for ordinary folk, for old wives and wabsters[6] (wives and weavers), in their homespun cloth. Surely this is one of the devil's champion lies! How unfortunate that it has found such acceptance! The infilling is what makes this promise true: *The one who is feeble among them in that day will be like David, and the house of David will be like God* (Zechariah 12:8), so that *one of your men puts to flight a thousand* (Joshua 23:10). This means defeat for the devil, so no wonder he strives to keep us back from the fullness of the Spirit!

We are here on earth so Christ may be glorified through us, but there is only One Person that can glorify

---

6   A possible reference to a line from a Robert Burns poem or a Scottish proverb.

Christ, and that is the Holy Spirit. *He will glorify Me* (John 16:14). The filling with the Spirit is necessary for the glorifying of Christ as he ought to be and might be glorified. Mothers in the home "by thronging duties pressed"[7] need the fullness to enable them to glorify Christ as surely as the apostles needed it; the woman who does laundry needs it as well as the pastor; the tradesman as well as the evangelist.

To live the Christ-glorifying life in the situation in which God has placed us, we individually need to be filled with the Spirit. *They were all filled* (Acts 2:4), men and women, the 120 in the upper room, the ordinary members as well as the apostles.

Repent, and each of you be baptized in the name of Jesus Christ for the forgiveness of your sins; and you will receive the gift of the Holy Spirit. For the promise is for you and your children and for all who are far off, as many as the Lord our God will call to Himself. (Acts 2:38-39)

From Acts 8:17 we conclude that *all* the converts in Samaria, without any favor or distinction, *received the Holy Spirit*. From Acts 10:47 we conclude that *all* in the house of Cornelius *received the Holy Spirit* while Peter was speaking. From Acts 19:6 we conclude that *the Holy Spirit came on* all the disciples to whom Paul was speaking. They all received because they all needed.

---

7   A reference to a line from a hymn titled "Peace, Perfect Peace" by Bishop Edward H. Bickersteth, 1875.

Don't we all need? Then why shouldn't we all receive? And if we don't receive we will suffer loss, the church will suffer loss, the world will suffer loss, and, above and beyond all, Christ will suffer loss.

Chapter 6

Preventing Backsliding

It is important to note how as soon as a man was converted, the early Christians were so eager that he should be filled with the Holy Spirit. They knew no reason why weary wastes of disappointing years should stretch between Bethel and Peniel, between the cross and Pentecost.

When Peter and John came to the Samaritans and found they had really turned to God, their first concern was to get them filled with the Holy Spirit (Acts 8:15). When Ananias came to the newly converted Saul of Tarsus, his first words were, *"Jesus . . . has sent me so that you may regain your sight and be filled with the Holy Spirit"* (Acts 9:17). When Paul found certain disciples at Ephesus, his first business with them was to find out if they had received the Holy Spirit (Acts 19:2). These early teachers did not wait for a few months or years until the young converts had become thoroughly disheartened because of the disappointments along the way, thoroughly demoralized by encountering defeats where they had been led to expect that they would be *more than conquerors* (Romans 8:37 JUB); neither did they wait until the novices had become more established or more fully instructed in the things of God. Instead, they immediately introduced them to fullness of blessing, taught them the open secret of the overcoming, ever-victorious life, and they did not leave them until the secret was their very own.

Has modern practice been aligned with apostolic practice in this respect? The only possible answer is in the negative. Have we improved, then, on the apostolic method? Scarcely. But our modern method is mainly responsible for the large percentage of backsliding that one meets with in the church today. Many of these backsliders were soundly converted to God, but unfortunately for them, no Peter or John, no Ananias or Paul met them in the beginning of their pilgrimage to compel their attention to the one thing necessary[8] for the people of the pilgrimage. So they started out but were unprepared, and after a longer or shorter time they became thoroughly discouraged, and then asking, "Is this all that is in it?" they threw their profession overboard.

---

8   The author's mention of "one thing needful" is a reference to Luke 10:42, an expression that many other writers of this era referenced as well.

One can scarcely wonder at it. Prevention is better than cure. Let's help our young converts to be fully instructed and fully equipped with the glorious fullness provided for them by the gracious Father, and we will hear less about backsliding. Do you know why Peter and John, and Ananias and Paul spoke of the fullness of the Spirit? Because they possessed and enjoyed the blessing themselves, and they could not but speak of the blessing that had done so much for them. Do you know why we have not spoken of it to our converts and young Christians? Because we did not know of it ourselves! If we receive the Spirit we will minister the Spirit, and if we do not minister, why is this? Only because we have not received.

Chapter 7

The Time between Regenerating and Filling

Peple often ask how much time must elapse between the regenerating by the Spirit and the filling with the Spirit. Remember, the filling is as real and distinct and definite of a blessing as the regenerating. Many people know the moment of their new birth; they were conscious of the change. In the same way, many know when they were filled with the Holy Spirit; it was a blessed, bright, conscious experience, and it is as impossible to argue them out of the one experience as out of the other.

On the other hand, some people do not know the time when they were born again; they simply have come to know by many reliable signs that the great change has taken place. So in a similar manner, some do not know when the fullness came to them, but they have been gently awakened to the fact that Jesus came, and he filled their soul. Such people may be as truly filled with the Spirit as those who can tell when and where and how the blessing came to them. About the period intervening between the two blessings, we know that in the case of the apostles in Acts 2:4, three or three and a half years elapsed between the day when they heard the "follow me" and the day when they were filled.

In the cases of the Samaritans in Acts 8:17 and of the Ephesians in Acts 19:1-7, some weeks passed. In the case of Saul in Acts 9:17, three days passed. But as we have already noticed in the case of Cornelius and his household in Acts 10:44, they were regenerated and filled in the same day. From this we conclude, as far as God is concerned, that there is no need for any intervening period, but the believer may be filled as soon as he is born again. The life may blossom into abundant life (John 10:10) almost as soon as we get it. If we did not receive the Holy Spirit when we believed, and if we have not received him since we believed, and we are not living the Spirit-filled life now, then at whose door does the blame fall?

Chapter 8

Other Words for Being
Filled with the Spirit

L et's glance at some other expressions used in the New Testament by the Holy Spirit when speaking of being Spirit-filled, so we can see how full the New Testament is of this blessing, and so we may better understand what it is and how it is obtained.

Baptized with the Holy Spirit

Scripture refers to it as being baptized with the Holy Spirit. *For John baptized with water, but you will be baptized with the Holy Spirit not many days from now* (Acts 1:5). For other examples of the same expression, see Acts 11:16, Matthew 3:11, Mark 1:8, Luke 3:16, and John 1:33.

Though *baptized* and *filled* are sometimes convertible

terms, it is important to note that they are not always so. The promise in Acts 1:5, *you will be baptized*, was fulfilled in Acts 2:4, *and they were all filled*, where *filled* is used for *baptized*. In Acts 4:8 we read, *Peter, filled with the Holy Spirit*, and in verse 31, *they were all filled with the Holy Spirit*, where the word *baptized* could not be used instead of the word *filled*. The difference is this: the "baptism" is received only once. It is like the initiatory rite to the life of Pentecostal service and fullness and victory. Life begins at the cross, but service begins at Pentecost. If there has been no baptism, there has been no Pentecost; and if there is no Pentecost, there is no service worth the name.

"Stay in the city until you are clothed with power from on high," said the Master (Luke 24:49). W*ait for what the Father had promised* (Acts 1:4). Y*ou will be baptized with the Holy Spirit not many days from now* (Acts 1:5). *You will receive power when the Holy Spirit has come upon you* (Acts 1:8). We see that in compliance with the commands of their Master, these men did not attempt service of any kind until *the day of Pentecost had come* (Acts 2:1).

Theirs not to make reply!

Theirs not to reason why![9]

Their business was simply to *obey*. With the promised baptism they entered into a new phase of life,

---

9   From "The Charge of the Light Brigade," a poem by Alfred Lord Tennyson.

experience, and service, and this baptism did not need to be repeated; but this is not the case with the filling.

Peter was filled in Acts 2:4 and again in Acts 4:31. The filling may be, and ought to be, repeated over and over again. The baptism need be only once. In support of this, note how frequently the word *filled* is used in Acts and the Epistles compared with the word *baptized.* The baptism which we are considering here must not be confused with the baptism in 1 Corinthians 12:13: *For by one Spirit we were all baptized into one body.* Paul is speaking there of every believer having been brought to life from the dead by the work of the Holy Spirit and thus made a member of Christ's mystical body. This is a Pauline way of stating the being *born again* of John 3:7.

It was to those who already had been *baptized into one body* that Christ gave the promise, *You will be baptized with the Holy Spirit* (Acts 1:5). In view, then, of this word of Christ, *You will be baptized,* and of the word of John the Baptist in John 1:29-33, *Behold the Lamb of God, who takes away the sin of the world. . . . this is the One who baptizes in the Holy Spirit* (the same promise is also recorded by Matthew, Mark, and Luke), it surely cannot be unscriptural for a believer to pray, "Lord Jesus, baptize me with the Holy Spirit," even if it is painfully obvious that this word has not yet been fulfilled in his experience, even if for him the day of Pentecost has yet not fully come. Why should this be regarded as unscriptural, when in view of the Word, *Be filled with the Spirit*, the prayer, "Lord, fill me with the Spirit," is considered to be in accord with Scripture? Surely the one prayer in its proper place is as scriptural as the other!

There are so many who know Christ as their sin-bearer who have no experiential acquaintance with him as the Baptizer with the Holy Spirit! We cannot miss the point that it would be grieving to the Holy One that such people would cry for the promised baptism, but then, when it has been received, let's keep in mind the difference already pointed out between baptized and filled. Let's remember that once *the day of Pentecost had come*, and a person has been baptized with the Spirit, he must not continue praying for the baptism, for that cannot be repeated, whereas he may ask and obtain a fresh filling, a refilling with the Holy Spirit every day of his life.

Rivers of Living Water

He who believes in Me, as the Scripture said, 'From his innermost being will flow rivers of living water.' But this He spoke of the Spirit, whom those who believed in Him

were to receive; for the Spirit was not yet
given, because Jesus was not yet glorified
(John 7:38-39).

One may ask what it is to be filled with the Spirit. The Teacher himself gives the answer: it is to have *rivers of living water* flowing from one's soul. Notice the universality of the promise, *He who believes in me*; no believer, even the weakest or obscurest, is outside of its magnificent sweep, unless by his unbelief he puts himself there. This is not a promise for the spiritual aristocracy of the church, as some maintain with more heat than sense. Let's have nothing to do with whittling away the vast godlike promises of the divine Word until they come within the cramped limits of our poverty-stricken experience, and let's earnestly set to work to bring our experience in line with God's promises.

This promise is for you. Then has it been verified in your life and experience? If not, why not? Isn't there a cause? But note more closely its hugeness, its godlike vastness. Rivers! Not a trickle or a babbling brook – by its babbling proclaiming its shallowness – or a stream, or a river, but rivers! What divine extravagance! It is the Brisbane, the Clarence, the Hawkesbury, the Murray, the Murrumbidgee, the Tamar, and the Derwent rivers all rolled into one. Rivers! By the widest, wildest stretch of the imagination could it be said of you that *rivers of living water* are flowing from you? Flowing – mind you – flowing.

Notice the freshness, the freedom, and the spontaneity of the service; there is no force pump involved in the flowing of the rivers – none of the hard labor of the soul in prison. When the rivers begin to flow, the worker may sell his force pump; his prayer has been answered: *Bring my soul out of prison* (Psalm 142:7).

It is worth noting the gradualness in the book of John. In John 3:7 we have life in its beginnings – the new birth called *born again*. In John 4:14 we have abundant life– *a well of water springing up*. The secret of the perpetual springing up is in the words *whoever drinks* – not takes one drink, but drinks and drinks and keeps on drinking. It is in the habit of drinking that someone never thirsts, for how can a man's soul be dry and thirsty with a well of water in it? Many people appear only to be reading the third chapter of John – they have life, but it is not strong and vigorous as is clearly presented in the fourth chapter.

The difference between the two experiences is well illustrated in the case of Hagar in Genesis. Here Abraham gave Hagar *a skin of water* and *sent her away* with her child. As she wandered in the wilderness, *the water in the skin was used up* and she had nothing left for her and her child (Genesis 21:14-15). She cried out to God, and in verse 19 we read, *God opened her eyes, and she saw a well of water; and she went and filled the skin with water.*

There are "bottle" Christians, and there are "well" Christians. Wandering in the wilderness with an empty bottle and a dying child is a painful experience! It is sad that there are so many familiar with the pain, when all the time God wants us to be independent of any bottle, to be abundantly satisfied with a well of water within us, fed from the hills of God. He wants us to be independent of everything but himself.

The well is in every Christian, though it is not springing up in every person who has it. The very well by which Jesus once sat beside, weary with his long journey, has no thirsty men or women coming to it with their empty pitchers today, for the well is dry. How? Why? Because so much rubbish has fallen in that the well is choked. Clear out the well, and the water will spring up again as it did in Christ's day.

This is how it is with so many children of God. The water is within them – the well is there – but it is choked; the water is not springing up, and so they are reduced to dependence on a bottle! Oh, to have anointed eyes in our heads to see the rubbish, and for grace in our hearts to deal with it, to judge it, and to cast it out. Then we would soon have eyes to see the well of water. May he break every bottle and open every eye to see the well.

Now let's contrast the well of the fourth chapter of

John with the rivers of the seventh chapter. The well is for the supply of all possible local needs, but since the Christianity of Jesus is essentially an unselfish thing, he has made abundant provision for the supply of surrounding needs. Out of the one who has the well – the one who is abundantly satisfied with Christ – *will flow rivers of living water* (John 7:38) bearing life, satisfaction, and gladness into the abounding death, destitution, and dreariness that exist all around us. For *everything will live where the river goes* (Ezekiel 47:9).

Does your church, your neighborhood, feel the life-giving, fruitful, refreshing influences of your presence? They most certainly will if John 7:38 is your experience – in other words, if you have been filled with the Spirit. But remember we must go through the experience in the fourth chapter of John to get into the seventh! In John 3 we have the indwelling, in John 4 the infilling, and in John 7 the overflowing.

The Promise of the Father

Baptism with the Holy Spirit is referred to as the promise of the Father. *Wait for what the Father had promised* (Acts 1:4). For more Scripture about this promise, see also Acts 2:33, 39; Galatians 3:14; Luke 24:49. There are many promises in the divine Word given us by the Father, but there is only one promise spoken of as *the* promise, which gives it a preeminence among all the other *precious and magnificent promises* (2 Peter 1:4). We can discover what that promise was by comparing Acts 1:4, *wait for what the Father had promised*, with Acts 1:5, *you will be baptized with the Holy Spirit*, and Acts 2:4, *they were all filled.*

To whom does the promise of the Father belong? Surely it belongs to all the Father's children without favor or distinction. Since, then, the promise is for you, the question for you to settle is, have you received the promise? A promise that is never made use of is like a check never cashed and is of little use to the one who gets it. Have you cashed the check? If not, why not? The fault is with the child and not with the Father.

Pouring Forth

The Bible calls the filling a pouring-out of the Spirit. *I WILL POUR FORTH OF MY SPIRIT ON ALL MANKIND* (Acts 2:17). See also Acts 2:18; Joel 2:28-29; Isaiah 44:3; Acts 2:33; Acts 10:45. From this expression we can learn even more clearly the copious nature of the blessing.

The Gift

Being filled with the Holy Spirit is a gift. *And you will*

receive the gift of the Holy Spirit (Acts 2:38). See also Acts 8:20; Acts 10:45; Acts 11:17. From this expression we can learn the freeness of the blessing. In this connection think carefully about the *how much more* Scripture talks about:

> *If you then, being evil, know how to give good gifts to your children, how much more will your heavenly Father give the Holy Spirit to those who ask Him?* (Luke 11:13)

Receiving

Being filled with the Holy Spirit involves receiving.

> *And they received the Holy Spirit.* (Acts 8:17)

> *You will receive power when the Holy Spirit has come upon you.* (Acts 1:8)

> *Did you receive the Holy Spirit when you believed?* (Acts 19:2)

Other passages that talk about receiving the Spirit include Acts 8:15; John 20:22; Galatians 3:14. Floods of light will shine on this subject if we clearly grasp the full force of this expression: Receive.

Receiving correlates with the gift. A gift will not benefit someone until it is received. It is here at the receiving that we have come short. God has not failed in his giving, but we have failed in our taking, in our receiving.

Receiving is a distinct, definite act on our part. Have we received? If not, why not? God is giving.

Falling On

Another expression for being filled with the Spirit is that he falls on us. *For He had not yet fallen upon any of them; they had simply been baptized in the name of the Lord Jesus* (Acts 8:16). See also Acts 10:44; Acts 11:15. From this expression, we can understand the suddenness with which the blessing sometimes comes, and comes consciously too. *And suddenly there came from heaven a noise like a violent rushing wind* (Acts 2:2).

Coming

The filling of the Holy Spirit might be described as "coming" on someone. *The Holy Spirit came on them* (Acts 19:6). See also Acts 1:8; John 16:7-8, 13. From this expression we can learn about the personality of the Holy Spirit. *Christ Jesus came into the world* (1 Timothy 1:15) and *the Holy Spirit came on them* are two parallel expressions. If it's clear here that Christ is a person, why should the Holy Spirit be a mere influence?

Sealed

Another way Scripture refers to the filling of the Spirit is as being *sealed*. *You were sealed in Him with the Holy Spirit of promise* (Ephesians 1:13). See also 2 Corinthians 1:22. This sealing in Ephesians 1:13 is the receiving mentioned in Acts 19:2 and the coming on them of Acts 19:6. Here in this epistle, Paul evidently refers to the incident relayed in Acts 19:1-7. In Ephesians 1:13 we read, *In Him, you also, after listening to the message of truth, the gospel of your salvation -having also believed, you were sealed in Him with the Holy Spirit of promise.* Here we see the successive stages through which the Ephesians passed in their spiritual history.

1) There was a time when they had not heard the gospel; they were living in the darkness of heathenism.

2) Then came the day when they heard the Word.

3) Then they believed.

4) After this they were sealed. This is a very distinct and definite blessing for the Ephesians, as definite as their salvation when they believed. And yet in the face of this, some will say that there is no such thing as a Christian receiving a new distinct blessing after his

conversion! If these Ephesians had this experience, why can't believers still have this today?

When a Christian is sealed by the Holy Spirit, sealed as the property of his Master, there will be no need to ask, "Whose image and superscription is this upon the sealed one?" It is the King's, of course. Anyone can see the image. Of what use is a seal if it can't be seen? Is the King's image visibly, permanently stamped upon us? It is on every Spirit-filled, sealed believer.

Chapter 9

How Is the Fullness Obtained?

We come now to the practical side of this subject. Surely the unprejudiced reader, if he has not already received the Holy Spirit, has at least come to the conclusion that there is such a blessing mentioned in the New Testament and waiting in God's Treasury, Jesus Christ, for all New Testament believers, and therefore for him, and for me. Until it dawns on one's consciousness that there is such a blessing as being filled with the Spirit, it is not likely that anyone will bother to seek it, and therefore will never obtain it.

In all fairness, these terms that we have just been considering – *filled*, *baptized*, *rivers*, etc. – mean something. There is some blessing represented by the terms, some substance behind the shadows. God the Holy Spirit knows what that blessing is. Do I have that? Is there anything in my life and experience to correspond with that? Now comes the question: How am I to get it? The Bible answer may be concisely understood in three words – *cleanse, consecrate, claim*. We will cover these three in the coming chapters.

Motives

Before proceeding to consider these words, it is absolutely necessary that we be on our guard against desiring such an important blessing from wrong motives. We must seek it for one supreme reason – for the glory of God. If self is at the root of our motives at all, God will most surely block our way to fullness of blessing. If we think that it would be a good thing for us to get this blessing for our own happiness or satisfaction, or even that we might be more useful, or that in any way we might have the preeminence, we are not sincere. *The eye is the lamp of the body; so then if your eye is clear, your whole body will be full of light* (Matthew 6:22).

Therefore, there is need for the refining fire to go through our heart. God must be Alpha and Omega in the matter. "For God's glory, and for God's glory alone" must be our motto as we proceed with our search for the fullness of the Spirit.

Chapter 10

Cleansing

In the same way that there are required conditions in order to obtain salvation (before someone can be justified) – for example, conviction of sin, repentance, and faith – there are also conditions for full salvation, for being filled with the Holy Spirit.

Conviction of our need is one; conviction of the existence of the blessing is another. But these have already been dealt with. Cleansing is another; before anyone can be filled with the Holy Spirit, their heart must be cleansed. *And God, who knows the heart, testified to them giving them the Holy Spirit, just as He also did to us; and He made no distinction between us and them, cleansing their hearts by faith* (Acts 15:8-9). God first cleansed their hearts, and then he gave them the Holy Spirit.

How can we be filled with the Holy Spirit if we

are filled with something else? The heart must first be emptied and cleansed. The milkman has called on his morning round, and the housewife hears his call. There is a jug standing beside her on the table; it is her own that she purchased only last week. She picks it up and looks into it to see if it is clean; she finds it is not. Now she would never think of taking that dirty jug for the milk, but she empties it and rinses and cleanses it, and then, having wiped it dry to her satisfaction, she takes it out for the morning portion.

If she brought the container out to the milkman dirty, he would positively refuse to put his sweet new milk into it. So a heart may belong to God, that is, it may be the heart of a Christian man, and yet not be a clean heart; until it is cleansed, God will refuse to put into it the precious deposit of the water of life, clear as crystal.

A "New Heart" Is Not Necessarily a Clean Heart

But someone objects, "I thought that when one became a Christian and was made a partaker of the divine nature, he had a clean heart."

Not necessarily. Many are born again, are pardoned and justified, and yet do not have a clean heart. Forgiveness is one thing and cleansing is another;

someone may possess the former without possessing the latter. For instance, take the case of David in Psalms. He was one of God's people, a restored backslider, when he wrote that psalm asking for a clean heart. *The LORD also has taken away your sin* (2 Samuel 12:13), Nathan said to him. But forgiveness, as great and sweet as that gift was, was not enough for Israel's now so deeply taught and penitent king.

Create in me a clean heart, O God, David cries (Psalm 51:10). This is something over and above being born again, over and above and beyond, and deeper even, than forgiveness (compare Psalm 51:2 and Jeremiah 33:8). See also the New Testament teaching on this point in 1 John 1:7, which says *the blood of Jesus His Son cleanses us from all sin,* and in 1 John 1:9 where we see *He is faithful and righteous to forgive us our sins and to cleanse us from all unrighteousness.* Is the cleansing of verse 7 the same as the cleansing of verse 9? Most certainly not.

The cleansing of verse 7 has to do with the guilt of sin, with sin after it has been committed. This is the only sense in which the blood of Jesus cleanses; it washes white as snow from the guilt and stain of actual transgression, and that cleansing is retrospective.

Now, this cleansing of verse 7 is the forgiving of verse 9; both of these words relate to a sinner's justification. But the cleansing from all unrighteousness of verse 9 is something different from, something over and above, the forgiving of verse 9 or the cleansing of verse 7. Otherwise, if they mean the same thing, wouldn't the author be guilty of redundancy?

The cleansing in verse 9 is prospective and refers to holiness of life, to our being saved from sin and from sinning. And you will notice that it is not the blood of Jesus that does this, but Jesus himself by the exercise of his almighty power. There is a great deal of confusion on this point in many minds, a confusion fostered, if not produced, by some of our hymns. Powers are sometimes attributed to the blood of Jesus – and to the death of Christ – that belong to Jesus himself, to the living Christ.

We are saved from sin's condemnation by the blood, cleansed from the guilt of all sin, forgiven on the grounds of the blood, and in this connection we cannot possibly make too much of the blood or too much of the death of the Son of God. But we are saved from sin's power by Jesus himself. *And you shall call His name Jesus, for He will save His people from their sins* (Matthew 1:21). *For if while we were enemies we were reconciled to God through the death of His Son, much more, having been reconciled, we shall be saved by His life* (Romans 5:10). *If we confess our sins, He is faithful and righteous to forgive us our sins and to cleanse us from all unrighteousness* (1 John 1:9).

Preventative Cleansing

The blood cleanses in the sense of washing the sin away after it has actually been committed; he cleanses in the sense of preventing and restraining from sin. He keeps us back from sinning. He makes us *more than conquerors* over sin (Romans 8:37 JUB); in this blessed sense, prevention is better than a cure. How often does a mother say to her child when putting on a clean, snow-white dress in the morning, "Now, my darling, do keep it clean!"

"Yes, mother," and she intends to do so, but unfortunately, despite her intentions, at dinnertime she comes home with her pinafore about as dirty as she can make it.

Now, the mother can wash it and make it clean again, as white as ever, but this everlasting washing is weary, wearing work. So the blood of Jesus can cleanse from all sin the garments that are brought to it for cleansing, and what a great deal of cleansing it has to do for some of us!

But wouldn't it be just splendid for a hardworking mother if she could put some power or other into her child – her own self, for instance – by which the child would be kept from making the pinafore dirty at all so that it would not need washing? Wouldn't this be a vast improvement, even on making it clean after it has been made dirty?

This is just what Jesus does. He puts a power within the child who trusts him; that power is himself, by which the believer is kept from defiling his garments by any known sin, so that they do not need washing. This is what it means to be *cleansed from all unrighteousness.* But there are whole battalions of God's saved, forgiven, and cleansed people (cleansed in the sense of 1 John 1:7) who are not cleansed in this sense (cleansed in the sense of verse 9), who are not yet saved from the power of some besetting (that is, constantly present or obsessive) sin or other.

Don't we know some Christians who, as has been well said, are like well-supplied cruet-stands?[10] Take of them whichever side you like and you will get something either hot or sour, peppery or vinegarish from them! And yet someone can scarcely doubt their conversion to God! What are we to say of these cross-grained, or fretful, or worldly-minded, or covetous, or pleasure-loving professors of religion? One would fear to judge some of them and say they were utter strangers to God's regenerating grace; no, but one *will* say that what they deeply need is a clean heart.

---

10 A cruet-stand is a small stand that holds salt and pepper shakers and often cruets or bottles of vinegar and olive oil.

What Is a Clean Heart?

The question then arises: What is it to have a clean heart? What is it to be *cleansed from all unrighteousness*? It is to be saved from our sins, according to Matthew 1:21. It is to translate 1 John 3:9 into practice: *No one who is born of God practices sin; . . . and he cannot sin, because he is born of God.* It is to have *a blameless conscience* (Acts 24:16). It is to be *conscious of nothing against myself* (1 Corinthians 4:4). It is – in the words of another – to be saved from all known, conscious sin.

"But," someone objects, "that is perfection!"

It is amazing how frightened some people are of being perfect! It would be good if they were equally afraid of being imperfect, for it is imperfection that grieves God. This dread of perfection has been called by someone "a scarecrow set up by the devil to frighten away God's people from the very finest of the wheat."

What we should want is the perfection that is not only allowed but also commanded in the Word of God. But it is not absolute perfection; it is not sinlessness. Let's look carefully at the expression "from all known, conscious sin." We're saved from all, yes, all, not some or nearly all, but from all known sin – that is, known to us, though not from all sin known to God; saved from all known, conscious sin so that one might be able to say, in the language of the lowliest of the apostles,

In view of this, I also do my best to maintain always a blameless conscience both before God and before men (Acts 24:16).

The lowliest of the apostles also said, *"For I am conscious of nothing against myself, yet I am not by this acquitted; but the one who examines me is the Lord"* (1 Corinthians 4:4). Or in the language of the disciple whom Jesus loved, *We keep his commandments and do the things that are pleasing in His sight* (1 John 3:22).

To have a clean heart, then, is to be saved from our sins, saved from sinning, saved by Jesus; take note of this! Not saved by our own efforts, by our watching and praying, or wrestling and fighting and struggling, but by Jesus. So it is not a question of what *we* can do, but of what *he* can do. *Is anything too difficult for the LORD?* (Genesis 18:14). Can't he *keep you from stumbling, and to make you stand in the presence of His glory blameless with great joy* (Jude 24)? Can't he save from sin and from sinning? Isn't this what is meant when it is said, *He is able also to save forever those who draw near to God through Him* (Hebrews 7:25)?

"Able to save," as Matthew Poole puts it, "to perfection, to the full, to all ends, from sin, in its guilt, its stain, its power." Yes, he is just as complete – as perfect – a Savior from the power of sin as he is from its guilt and stain. He is equally powerful in each department of his saving work. But after all is said and done and someone is being saved from all known, conscious sin – saved from sinning – this is not to say there is no sin remaining. We are face to face with the inspired statement, *If we say that we have no sin, we are deceiving ourselves* (1 John 1:8). How much sin might there be in us that we are entirely unconscious of, but which is naked and open to those *eyes like a flame of fire* (Revelation 2:18)!

A Clean Conscience

I am conscious of nothing against myself, cries Paul in 1 Corinthians 4:4, *yet I am not by this acquitted; but the one who examines me is the Lord.* God may, and does, know much against me when I know nothing against myself; it is exactly here that our constant need of the cleansing blood comes in.

If the Bible doctrine of the clean heart meant the eradication of sin, a state of sinlessness – that is, absolute perfection – then what need would we have for the cleansing blood at all? Though Jesus Christ may have cleansed *us from all unrighteousness,* so that we have *a blameless conscience,* so that we have nothing on our conscience, yet we need the blood to cleanse from the sins our eyes fail to detect and of which our conscience has no awareness. It is failure to see this that has led many astray at this point.

Having been cleansed and having *no more conscience*

of sin (Hebrews 10:2 JUB), they imagine they have no more sin. How superficial some people's idea of sin is. How little conception they have of the Pauline doctrine of sin! He speaks of sin as *utterly sinful* (Romans 7:13). How subtle it is. How far-reaching!

In their daring ignorance some have actually taken the penknife, like Judah's foolish king, and cut a whole petition out of the prayer the Lord taught his disciples. He taught them to pray, *And forgive us our debts, as we also have forgiven our debtors* (Matthew 6:12), but these modern lights in their darkness are correcting their Teacher and have cut out that petition and thrown it away.

"We have no need to confess our sin, for we have none to confess, and therefore we have no debts to be forgiven."

Poor mistaken people! There is never more need of confession and forgiveness than when they are speaking this way! The holiest of men are the ones who lie the lowest before the Holy One confessing that which they know only too well (because the truth is in them), that they "have sin," offering the sacrifices with which God is ever well pleased: *a broken spirit; A broken and a contrite heart* (Psalm 51:17). The nearer we get to the One whose *hair were white like white wool, like snow* (Revelation 1:14), to the Ancient of Days, *His vesture was like white snow And the hair of His head like pure wool* (Daniel 7:9), the more conscious are we of the dullness of our whiteness, of the vast difference between our whitest and his whiteness, and this consciousness humbles a person.

Short of Glory

"What is it to have sin? What is sin?" a great leader once asked, and he answered his own question this way: "It is to come short of the glory of God, and in this sense we sin every moment of our lives in thought, word, and deed." Is there a man on earth who can stand before the infinitely Holy One and say, "I do not come short of your glory"? If we speak this way, *we are deceiving ourselves and the truth is not in us* (1 John 1:8).

We may be helped here by observing the difference between the two New Testament words *blameless* and *faultless.*

> *Now may the God of peace Himself sanctify you entirely; and may your spirit and soul and body be preserved complete, without blame at the coming of our Lord Jesus Christ.* (1 Thessalonians 5:23)

This is to be preserved without blame. *To make you stand in the presence of His glory blameless with great joy* (Jude 24). A person or work may be blameless and yet not be faultless. This is not verbal hairsplitting – by no means.

Bear with me for a personal illustration. I have a letter lying on the table beside me, which will illustrate the point at hand. I received it when I was away in New Zealand on a mission tour in 1891. It was from my eldest daughter, then a child of five years of age. It reads, "Dear father, I wrote all this myself. I send you a kiss from Elsie." The fact of the matter is, that it is not writing at all, but an attempt at printing in large capitals, and not one of the letters is properly formed; there is not as much as one straight stroke on the page. Why is it that I prize this letter and keep it stored away among my treasures? Fathers who are away from home as much as I am will understand when I say that it was my child's first attempt at letter writing. Now, this letter that I prize so dearly is certainly not a faultless production; it is as full of faults as it is full of letters. But it is most assuredly blameless.

I did not blame my child for her crooked strokes and answer her with a scold, for I judged her work by its motive. I knew it was the best she could do and that she had put all the love of her little heart into it. She wanted to do something to please me, and she succeeded. By the grace of the indwelling Christ – for you will perceive that it is his work, *Faithful is He who calls you, and He also will bring it to pass* (1 Thessalonians 5:24) – this is what our daily life, our daily lifework, may be, namely, that we are blameless. And he can tell us that it is, even as I told my child, so we may have this testimony: that we are pleasing God, as Enoch was (Hebrews 11:5).

Without Blemish or Fault

Oh, the joy! Oh, the inspiration of this God-given testimony! But what a sad mistake for anyone who may have been made blameless by grace, to think they are faultless, a condition that is to be found only before the throne, *in the presence of his glory* (Jude 24). For it is to be noted that the Greek word *amomos*, translated *without blemish* and *without fault* is never used of God's people on earth. It is used once of the Lamb *unblemished and spotless* (1 Peter 1:19). Elsewhere it is used of the saints.

In Revelation 14:5, *they are unblemished before the throne of God.*

In Jude 24, *Now to Him who is able to keep you from stumbling, and to make you stand in the presence of His glory blameless with great joy.*

In Ephesians 5:27, *having no spot or wrinkle or any such thing; but that she would be holy and blameless* when in the sweet by-and-by he will present the church to himself.

In Ephesians 1:4, *just as He chose us in Him before the foundation of the world, that we would be holy and blameless before Him. In love;* chosen in the past eternity that we should be *holy and unblemished* in the coming eternity – not here, but there. Not now, but then. For the word translated as *before* is the same Greek word *katenopion* that is translated in Jude 24 as *before the presence of.*

In Colossians 1:22, *to present you holy and blameless and beyond reproach.* Here he is speaking again of our future standing, because the word translated *before* is the same as in Ephesians 1:4.

Without blemish, then, is sinlessness, having no sin. *If we say [here on earth] that we have no sin [are sinless – without blemish, faultless, flawless], we are deceiving ourselves [but no one else!], and the truth is not in us* (1 John 1:8). The person who has the truth in him knows only too well that he has sin in him, though he is cleansed from all sin by the blood, and though he is *cleansed from all unrighteousness* by the might of the uttermost Savior.

It is most important and humbling to notice how the Spirit of truth has placed that part – *If we say that we have [present tense] no sin, we are deceiving ourselves* – in between his two statements about the cleansing *from all sin* and the cleansing *from all unrighteousness.*

But though we will never be able on earth to say

with the truth in us that we have no sin – that we are without blemish – yet the whole Bible teaches us that in this life we may be saved from our sins. (Note the difference between *sin* and *sins*.) We may be saved from sinning. *I am writing these things to you so that you may not sin* (1 John 2:1); this is the condition described as blameless, unreproveable, and without reproach.

See where the Greek word *anegkletos* (unreproveable) is used in 1 Corinthians 1:8; 1 Timothy 3:10; Titus 1:6-7.

Also see 1 Timothy 3:2 and 5:7 where the Greek word is *anepileptos* (without reproach).

See Matthew 12:5 where *anaitios* (guiltless) is used.

See 2 Peter 3:14 where *amometos* (blameless) is employed.

Also see where *amemptos* (without blame) is the word used in Luke 1:6; Philippians 2:15; 3:6; 1 Thessalonians 2:10; 3:13; 5:23.

Blameless, Not Faultless

These words describe a state or condition of heart and life that is not only attainable here, but is also imperative, and the passages we have just been reading prove that it has been attained. This is what is meant by a clean heart – to be blameless, not faultless.

I was sitting alone in the twilight,
    With spirit troubled and vexed,
With thoughts that were morbid and gloomy,
    And faith that was sadly perplexed.

Some homely work I was doing
    For the child of my love and care;
Some stitches half wearily setting
    In the endless need of repair.

But my thoughts were about the building,
    The work some day to be tried,
And that only the gold and the silver,
    And the precious stones should abide

And remembering my own poor efforts,
    The wretched work I had done,
And even when trying most truly,
    The meager success I had won:

It is nothing but wood, hay and stubble.
    I said, "It will all be burned;
This useless fruit of the talents
    One day to be returned;

And I have *so* longed to serve Him,
    And sometimes I know I have tried;
But I'm sure when He sees such building
    He will never let it abide."

Just then as I turned the garment,
    That no rent should be left behind,
Mine eye caught an odd little bungle
    Of mending and patchwork combined

My heart grew suddenly tender,
    And something blinded mine eyes
With one of those sweet inspirations,
    That sometimes make us so wise.

Dear child! she wanted to help me,
    I knew 'twas the best she could do;
But oh! what a botch she had made of it
    The gray mismatching the blue!

And yet, can you understand it?
    With a tender smile and a tear,
And a half compassionate yearning,
    I feel her grow more dear.

Then a sweet voice broke the silence,
    And the dear Lord said to me,
"Art thou tenderer for thy little child
    Than I am tender for thee?"

Then straightway I knew His meaning,
    So full of compassion and love;
And my faith came back to its refuge
    Like the glad returning dove.

So, I thought, when the Master Builder
    Comes down this temple to view,
To see what rents must be mended,
    And what must be builded anew,

Perhaps, as He looks o'er the building
    He will bring my work to the light;
And seeing the marring and bungling,
    And how far it is all from right;

He will feel as I felt for my darling,
    And will say as I said for her,
"Dear child! she wanted to help me,
    And love for Me was the spur;

And for the great love that is in it
    The work shall seem perfect as mine;
And, because it was willing service,
    Will crown it with plaudit divine."

And there, in the deepening twilight,
    I seemed to be clasping a hand,
And to feel a great love constraining,
    Far stronger than any command.

Then I knew by the thrill of sweetness,
    'Twas the Hand of the Blessed One
Which should tenderly guide and hold me,
    Till all the labor is done.

So my thoughts are never more gloomy,
My faith is no longer dim,
But my heart is strong and restful,
And mine eyes are unto Him.[11]

A clean heart does not mean sinlessness, eradication of sin, or that sin is taken out of us. For although sin is taken out of the heart that is cleansed (for a clean heart must be clean), the flesh, the self-life, still remains in the person. It is latent, if not patent,[12] ready to manifest itself should the counteracting power of the indwelling Christ the Savior be withdrawn for even a moment. This flesh is evil (Romans 7:18), and therefore while the flesh is in us, sin is in us; hence our constant need of the cleansing blood.

As we trust for continuous cleansing we get it. The *blood cleanses* – present progressive tense – it goes on cleansing; therefore, guilt is never allowed to gather, for as sin appears, the blood cleanses it away and so keeps us clean. Blessed present tense! Thus it is possible for us always to walk in the light.

Then as Christ exercises his counteracting power over the flesh, we are being cleansed from all unrighteousness, delivered from doing the "not right," and by continuous trust in our omnipotent Savior, we may

---

11   A poem titled "A Voice in the Twilight" by Katharine Hardenbergh Johnson.

12   *Latent* means it is hidden or concealed, but a *patent* flaw is obvious or already known.

know continuous deliverance and continuous victory over sin; we never need to know defeat.

Victory

A Christian mother had just kissed her little daughter good-night and was busy in the dining room arranging the table for dinner, when she heard little feet on the stairs. Wondering what was the matter, she slipped into the window recess and hid herself behind the curtains and waited. After a little while, the little one came into the room, went straight up to some peaches that were on the table, and she took one of them away with her.

Oh, the agony in that mother's heart. She did not speak to her child, but standing where she was, she spoke to God her Father and asked him so fervently to speak to her child. God heard that cry, and in a little while the sound of the pattering feet was heard on the stair again. The child came into the room, not knowing her mother was there, and went on tiptoe over to the table, where she put the peach in the place from which she had taken it. She turned away with a radiant face, rubbing her hands with delight.

That's victory! Yes, the cleansing means that and more than that. *We are more than conquerors*, for when Jesus cleanses the heart, he cleanses the springs of our action and our being, so that our very desires are purified; the desire to sin, the "want to," is taken clean away. This is coming off *more than conquerors through him that loved us* (Romans 8:37 JUB). Glory to his name! The man now wants to do the will of God. He likes what God likes.

"I thought you could do what you liked," a young man hurled this taunt at a friend of his who enjoyed full salvation, when that friend refused to go to the theater. "I thought you told me you could do what you liked."

"So I can."

"Why, then, won't you come with me as I asked you?"

"Because I don't like," was the response.

The only people on earth who enjoy perfect freedom are those who have clean hearts, for they not only know that they ought to do the will of God, but they also want to do it and they like to do it; and furthermore, they have a power that enables them to do it. On the other hand, in our jails and hospitals you will find people who thought they could do as they liked, but they have discovered they were mistaken.

Cleansing: An Act in the Moment

Some may wonder, but how am I to get this clean heart? Peter answers, *And He made no distinction between us and them, cleansing their hearts by faith* (Acts 15:9). Cleansing is God's work, and the condition on which

God will do his work is faith on our part. There is only one way of getting anything from God and that is by faith.

We obtain forgiveness and the new birth by faith, and we obtain cleansing of the heart by faith too. You may, and you will, get cleansing the moment you definitely trust Christ for it. "We aye get what we gang in for," was one of Duncan Mathieson's favorite expressions; along the line of God's revealed will, how true it is!

If you will only trust in Christ for cleansing from all unrighteousness, he will do it for you now. *Woe to you, O Jerusalem! How long will you remain unclean?* (Jeremiah 13:27). Why not now? Cleansing is a crisis (an act in the moment) and not a process, but as Principal Moule of Cambridge[13] has very tersely put it, "Cleansing is a crisis with a view to a process."

It is just here that multitudes of God's people miss the track. "Sanctification is the work of God's free grace."[14] Of course it is. It is a growth, a gradual process, but cleansing is not sanctification. The latter, in the sense in which it is being used here, is a theological term that embraces all the Spirit's work in the believer between the cross and the crown. But cleansing is an action. While sanctification is a growth, cleansing is one of the conditions of growth. The very reason why

---

13 Handley Carr Glyn Moule (1841–1920) was an evangelical Anglican theologian and writer.

14 Westminster Shorter Catechism, Question 35

some who hold most firmly to the theory of gradual sanctification are growing in grace so very slowly is because they have not attended to one of the most essential conditions for growth, namely, this cleansing.

"But," someone objects, "this is not in the standards of our church." That may be, but it is in the Bible.

To quote the words of the saintly Dr. Andrew Bonar:[15] "I believe all that is in our standards, for I find all that is in our standards in the Bible; but I believe more than is in our standards, for I find some things in my Bible that are not in the standards." The point is the simple and very obvious reason that you cannot get a quart into a pint measure. While every honest churchman believes that all that is in the standards of the church to which he belongs is in the Bible, no one in his sane senses believes that everything in the Bible is to be found in the standards. The doctrine of a clean heart is one of these things.

In support of the statement that cleansing is a crisis, an act – something done in a moment the same way as conversion is – and not a process drawn out indefinitely before one can reach a state of cleansing, let's think over David's prayer in Psalm 51:10: *Create in me a clean heart.* Is creation an act or a work? Is it a crisis or a process? All the Creator had to do was to speak the word and David's prayer was granted, and then he

---

15 Dr. Andrew Alexander Bonar (1810–1892) was a minister of the Free Church of Scotland.

could turn his prayer into thanksgiving. "I thank Thee for having created in me a clean heart." But he could not thank God for what he had not received.

Giving thanks for the clean heart would prove that it was in his possession. Note also that heart cleansing is God's work alone. We are exhorted to *cleanse ourselves from all defilement of flesh and spirit* (2 Corinthians 7:1), which simply means separation from all the palpable, manifest evils Paul had just been listing, such as yoking with unbelievers, unrighteousness, communion with darkness, affiliation with Belial (the devil), and unfaithful people, idols, and unclean things (see 2 Corinthians 6:14-17). In reference to all such things, God says, *cleanse* yourselves.

The aorist tense[16] used in the original Greek denotes a definite, decisive act: separate from these things at once and be done with them. And where are we to get the enabling power? In effect, God says, "Draw a check on me; draw on my resources for all you need," for all God's commands are God's enabling. But when it comes to be a question of cleansing the heart, the inner being, the springs of action, that part of the person where the affections and the will are seated, God manages that himself. He says, "Bring that to me."

If this work were left to us it would be a slow and tedious process for sure, and progress might be made

---

16   A form of a verb in some languages, such as Classical Greek, that expresses action without indicating its completion or continuation.

backwards, as unfortunately it so often is. But now the question is not what can the believer do by his efforts to overcome indwelling sin, but what can the almighty God do? It is not a question of our power, but of his.

> 'Twas most impossible of all,
>   That here sin's reign in me should cease;
> Yet shall it be! I know it shall;
>   Jesus, look to Thy faithfulness;
> If nothing is too hard for Thee,
>   All things are possible to me.[17]

He is able and willing to cleanse. Are we willing to be cleansed?

A Means to an End

Another mistake to be carefully guarded against is our making cleansing to be an end instead of a means to an end. Cleansing is not the blessing that we seek; it is only a means. The end is the filling of the Holy Spirit. Cleansing is a negative blessing – the separating from sin – but we can only be satisfied with a positive blessing. When the housewife cleans the house, does she go out afterward and live in the yard? No. She cleans the house so it may be the more fit for her to inhabit.

---

17 A verse of a hymn by Charles Wesley (1707-1788) titled "All Things Are Possible to Him."

God cleanses, empties, sweeps, and garnishes (Matthew 12:44) that he may come in to dwell, and if he, the Holy One, does come in and take up his residence, he will keep his dwelling place clean. This cleansing of which we have been speaking is one of the steps into the blessed life, but there is not much likelihood of anyone living the life unless they first take the necessary steps into the life. It is a life of purity, and it is lived, as it is entered upon, by faith in the Son of God, hence the name by which the Spirit-filled life is sometimes called – the life of faith.

Chapter 11

Consecration

Before fullness can be obtained, the second step that needs to be taken by those of us who have been living without it is consecration, a word that is very common and popular, much more common and popular, it is feared, than the thing itself. In order to be filled with the Holy Spirit one must first be cleansed and then one must be consecrated. Consecration follows cleansing, and not vice versa. Intelligent comprehension of what consecration is and of what it involves is necessary for an intelligent consecration of oneself.

Sanctification

Consecration is another word for sanctification. Many people are confused about what sanctification really is.

We must bear in mind that we are not considering

the theological term *sanctification*, but the use of the New Testament word *sanctify* or *sanctification*. No one would confuse consecration with cleansing, and yet many confuse sanctification with cleansing. They tell us that to sanctify is to purify, to cleanse, or to make holy. But the idea of purification, of cleansing, of separating from sin, is not in the New Testament word *sanctify* at all.

Now may the God of peace Himself sanctify you entirely (1 Thessalonians 5:23). That does not mean purify you or separate you from sin, as a glance at two other passages in which the same word occurs will show. *For their sakes I sanctify Myself* (John 17:19). *Sanctify Christ as Lord in your hearts* (1 Peter 3:15). Here it cannot mean purify or separate from sin. In these passages its true meaning is very apparent – to set apart for a holy use, to separate to God, to consecrate.

To cleanse is to separate *from* sin, but to sanctify is to separate *to* God – to set apart for God that which has already been separated from sin. We cannot set apart to a holy use (consecrate) that which is not cleansed. Hence, we see why it is that cleansing must precede sanctification or consecration, *that He might sanctify her, having cleansed her [Greek ekklesia – "called out ones"] by the washing of water with the word* (Ephesians 5:26).

Sanctification is not identical to cleansing, but it is its complement. *We have been sanctified through the offering of the body of Jesus Christ once for all* (Hebrews 10:10). *Therefore Jesus also, that He might sanctify the people through His own blood, suffered outside the gate* (Hebrews 13:12). From these passages we gather that it is by the blood of Jesus we are sanctified – set apart to God. This is another function of the precious blood in addition to the one we have already been considering, namely, cleansing from the guilt of sin.

Surrender

"In conversion," says Dr. Chalmers,[18] "God gives to me, but in consecration I give to God." Most people know that conversion should be acquainted with consecration.

> In full and glad surrender,
> I give myself to thee.[19]

Consecration involves surrender – total, absolute, unconditional, and irreversible. This is Paul's teaching in Romans: *Therefore I urge you, brethren, by the mercies of God, to present your bodies a living and holy sacrifice, acceptable to God, which is your spiritual service of worship.* (Romans 12:1). These people had already given their souls to God, and now the apostle insists

---

18 Possibly Scottish minister, Thomas Chalmers (1780–1847).
19 From a hymn by Frances Ridley Havergal (1836–1879), titled "In Full and Glad Surrender."

on their giving their bodies too. *Present [the KJV says "yield"] yourselves to God as those alive from the dead* (Romans 6:13). Life first, then sacrifice. Do we have life in Christ? Then it is imperative that we yield, or present, ourselves to God.

It is not a matter of individual choice or taste or convenience, but everyone who has been revived from the death in trespasses and sins is commanded – yes, commanded – to present themselves to God. Have you obeyed this command? If not, why not? God excuses no one. Shouldn't you attend to it now? Yes, before you read another line!

It follows as a result that if we yield ourselves, we yield everything else to God; nothing is withheld. What loss we suffer because we will hold back some little thing! A little child was once playing with a valuable vase, and he put his hand into it and could not pull it back out. His father also tried his best to get it out, but all in vain.

They were talking of breaking the vase when the father said, "Now, my son, make one more try; open your hand and hold your fingers out straight, as you see me doing, and then pull."

To their astonishment the little fellow said, "Oh no, Pa. I couldn't put out my fingers like that, for if I did, I would drop my penny."

He had been holding on to a penny all the time!

No wonder he could not remove his hand. How many of us are like him! Drop the copper, surrender, let go, and God will give you gold.

Now let's note that the verb translated in the King James Version as *yield* in Romans 6:13 and *present* in Romans 12:1 is not in the present tense in the original, which would be as if Paul had said "be yielding," "keep presenting." Instead, it is in the aorist tense, which means the general emphasis is on a definite act having been done and finished. So when the command to present yourself to God is obeyed as far as one's understanding goes, the person is entitled to regard the transaction as a completed act and to say, "Yes, I have presented myself to God."

Then faith presses on the heels of that statement and says, "God has accepted what I have thus presented. It is absolutely necessary that faith be in action on this point, for what will be the practical outcome of all my presenting if I do not believe that God takes what I give? *The one who comes to Me I will certainly not cast out* (John 6:37) is just as appropriate to the saint seeking full salvation as to the sinner seeking pardon. It is failure here – failure to apprehend by faith the fact that God receives what I present – that has blocked progress for so many of God's people who truly desire to live consecrated lives.

From this we can see that consecration is a crisis

(a moment) in the life of the believer, just as cleansing is. It is not a process, but it too is a crisis that leads to a process.

Transference of Ownership

Consecration implies and involves transference of ownership. Many a Christian today lives as if he belongs to himself, but the consecrated heart endorses the statement of the divine Word: *Or do you not know that your body is a temple of the Holy Spirit who is in you, whom you have from God, and that you are not your own? For you have been bought with a price: therefore glorify God in your body* (1 Corinthians 6:19-20). The consecrated person looks upon himself as the absolute property of the Lord who bought him, and his whole life is lived in the light of this fact.

Enthroning Christ

Consecration involves the glorifying of Christ, the enthroning him, the crowning of Jesus as Lord of all in our own heart and life. "Crown Him, crown Him, Lord of all"[20] and, says Dr. Hudson Taylor, "If you do not crown Him Lord of all you do not crown Him Lord

---

20   From the hymn "All Hail the Power of Jesus' Name" by Edward
      Perronet (1726-1792).

at all." This view of consecration, with its accompanying results, is beautifully illustrated for us in Scripture:

He who believes in Me, as the Scripture said, 'From his innermost being will flow rivers of living water.' But this He spoke of the Spirit, whom those who believed in Him were to receive; for the Spirit was not yet given, because Jesus was not yet glorified (John 7:38-39).

The flowing forth of the rivers – just the outflow, the overflow of the infilling Spirit – was dependent on Jesus being glorified. Jesus had not yet reached the throne, and so the Spirit had not yet been given. The reason why they had not come to Pentecost was that as yet there was no ascension. Ascension preceded Pentecost.

Let's learn it by root of heart that every Pentecost since the first has, in similar manner, been preceded by an ascension. Have we experienced Pentecost for ourselves? If not, the reason is close at hand.

Jesus has not been glorified by us, not enthroned in our hearts. He may be in the heart – he may even be in the throne room – but he has not been placed upon the throne! There has never been a coronation day in our lives, when "in full and glad surrender" we placed the crown on the many-crowned head, crying, "Crown Him, crown Him, Lord of all!"[21]

Then he showed me a river of the water of

---

21   See previous notes in this chapter about the two hymns quoted.

*life, clear as crystal, coming from the throne
of God and of the Lamb.* (Revelation 22:1)

When Christ reached the throne at the Father's right
hand, the river began to flow from underneath his
throne, the Holy Spirit was given, and his church
received her Pentecost. *Therefore having been exalted
to the right hand of God. . . He has poured forth this
which you both see and hear* (Acts 2:33). So when Christ
is exalted, enthroned, and glorified in the believer's
heart, the rivers will begin to flow from underneath
his throne according to promise; but no ascension, no
Pentecost. Let's remember, as has been already stated,
that though life begins at the cross, service does not
begin till Pentecost. No Pentecost, no service worthy
of the name!

We do not need to be concerned with how the rivers flow from us or be troubled about what channels
they flow in. They flowed from Peter in one way and
from Paul in quite another, and from Barnabas in yet
another; there are infinite varieties of ways. We do
not need to be troubled at all about the rivers and the
direction of their flow; our concern is to glorify Jesus,
to see that he is on the throne, and then it becomes
his business to see that the rivers are flowing. There is
not the slightest danger that the blessed business with
which he charges himself will be neglected!

There are other aspects of consecration in the divine Word which have not been touched upon, but enough has been said for our purpose to show what it is and what its blessed results will be. Our life and service will be enriched beyond telling by enthroning Christ. This, of course, involves the breaking of all our idols, for he will not share his throne with any.

When Mahmoud,[22] the conqueror of India, had taken the city of Gujarat, as was his custom he proceeded to destroy the idols. There was one, fifteen feet high, that its priests and devotees begged him to spare. He was deaf to their appeals and seizing a hammer he struck it with one blow; to his amazement, from the shattered image a shower of gems, pearls, and diamonds rained down at his feet – treasure of fabulous value that had been hidden within it! Had he spared the idol he would have lost all this wealth.

Let us not spare our idols. It is to our benefit to demolish them. If we shatter them, the very treasures of heaven will rain into our hearts – the gifts and graces of the Holy Spirit. But if we spare our idols, we will miss unfathomable riches.

The consecrated life is a Christ-centered life, the only truly centered life; every other life is eccentric. Yet how often do we hear worldly people or worldly minded Christians (what a contradiction in terms!)

---

22   Also spelled Mahmud. In AD 998, the Turkish conqueror, Mahmud of Ghazni, established an empire in Central Asia.

criticizing some devoted Spirit-filled man or woman as "so eccentric," simply because of their loyalty to Christ their King, when all the while it is the critics who are eccentric – off the true center. Indeed, the first Spirit-filled crew appeared so eccentric that *Others were mocking and saying, "They are full of sweet wine"* (Acts 2:13). So they were full of new wine, the new wine of the kingdom. And in God's sight, these drunken, eccentric men were the only truly centered, spiritually adjusted men in the crowd.

Chapter 12

Claiming

Having considered the two conditions that are necessary for being filled with the Spirit – the cleansing of the heart and the consecration of the cleansed heart to God – we come now to the very practical question: How is this fullness to be obtained by the cleansed and consecrated believer? Before proceeding to consider the answer – claim it – let's notice what the divine Word has to say about prayer and laying on of hands in connection with this obtaining.

Prayer

How much more will your heavenly Father give the Holy Spirit to those who ask Him? (Luke 11:13)

This promise is given to God's children. It is the dearest wish of the great Father-heart of God that his children would be filled with his Spirit. Who has a fathoming line – a depth finder – long enough to measure the depths of that "how much more"? You ask, the Father gives. What is the next step? Why, of course, you receive! Otherwise all the Father's giving will be of no use.

> *When they had prayed, . . . they were all filled with the Holy Spirit.* (Acts 4:31)

> *Who, . . . prayed for them that they might receive the Holy Spirit.* (Acts 8:15)

Stay (Luke 24:49). *Wait* (Acts 1:4). This is not idling, but praying, pleading the promise, as *these all with one mind were continually devoting themselves to prayer* (Acts 1:14). *they were all together in one place. And suddenly . . .* the answer came (Acts 2:1-2)! So in obtaining the blessing of the fullness, prayer has its place.

Laying on of Hands

> *Then they began laying their hands on them, and they [the Samaritan converts] were receiving the Holy Spirit.* (Acts 8:17)

Then, when they had fasted and prayed and laid their hands on them, they sent them away. (Acts 13:3)

Barnabas and Saul were men who were already full of the Holy Spirit, but by the laying on of hands (it is probable that hands had been laid on these men before this) they received a fresh anointing of the Holy Spirit – a fresh equipment for special service – and thus they were set apart for the work to which the Holy Spirit was calling them.

And when Paul had laid his hands upon them [the men of Ephesus], the Holy Spirit came on them. (Acts 19:6)

And after praying, they laid their hands on them [the deacons]. (Acts 6:6)

Do not neglect the spiritual gift within you, which was bestowed on you through prophetic utterance with the laying on of hands by the presbytery. (1 Timothy 4:14)

Kindle afresh the gift of God which is in you through the laying on of my hands. (2 Timothy 1:6)

It is quite evident that laying on of hands was no meaningless ceremony in the primitive church. Is there any reason why it should ever be an empty, barren form in our own day?

We come now to examine the answer given to the question: How is the fullness of the Spirit to be obtained? The answer is, claim it. We must clearly bear in mind that we now deal with a cleansed and consecrated soul. If you are not cleansed, attend to that cleansing first. If you are not consecrated, attend at once to the consecrating, and then – but not until then – will you be able to profit by what will be said about the claiming of the blessing.

Do we understand the immense difference between claiming and asking? I *claim* that which is my own; I *ask* for a favor. For instance, if a man has a credit balance of $250 in his current banking account, and he writes a check for $50, he does not need to go to the manager and ask for $50; he presents his check and claims it, for it is his own. But suppose that same man is in need of an advance of $500. He goes into the banker's office and asks for the favor of a loan. No claiming now!

So it often is with the Christian and his God. When God gives a definite promise for some definite blessing, it is the Christian's privilege to claim – to receive by faith – the thing that is promised. If God tells him a certain blessing is his by virtue of his sonship, it is his to claim, to receive what has been made his own through grace. There is no asking needed here – that is, asking in the sense of saying, "Lord, if it is your holy will, give me this."

Where is the room for an if? Hasn't God told him it is his will? Hasn't he promised it? Hasn't he given it to him? Then why should he mock his Lord by saying, "If it is your will"?

On the other hand, suppose that man wants something that God has not expressly promised to give, something in reference to which he has not revealed his will. All the Christian can do in this case is to ask; he cannot claim. God may give him what he asks, or he may see that it will be for the best to refuse his child's request.

A Christian may want $250 and may ask his Father to send it to him, and God may give or withhold. But if a Christian wants to be filled with the Holy Spirit, he or she needs to have no doubt about the issue here; they may claim the fullness, for hasn't God promised it? Isn't this blessing his very own? His birthright by virtue of his new birth?

Let's learn, then, to clearly distinguish between claiming as an act of faith based on an express promise in the Word, and asking as a request in prayer. It is abundantly clear from the Word of God that the fullness of the Holy Spirit is one of the blessings that it is our privilege to claim, to receive by a simple act of faith.

> *Christ redeemed us from the curse of the Law, having become a curse for us- for it is written, "CURSED IS EVERYONE WHO HANGS ON A TREE "- in order that in Christ Jesus the blessing of Abraham might come to the Gentiles, so that we would receive the promise of the Spirit through faith.* (Galatians 3:13-14)

The double purpose of Christ's redeeming work, of his being made a curse for us, is plainly stated here. He was cursed that we might be blessed with a double blessing – first with *the blessing of Abraham*, that is, righteousness and justification; second with *the promise of the Spirit*. So many of God's children forget the second blessing! They think that if they are saved from wrath and justified, that is all.

Have we overlooked this fact? Have we been stopping short? Those who do not live the Spirit-filled life void the work Christ accomplished on the tree to a most alarming extent, as far as they are personally concerned. Christ died that we might be made the righteousness of God, and that we might be filled with God. As God holds the sinner guilty who neglects this great salvation and rejects the offered righteousness, so he holds the justified believer guilty who neglects the second blessing that Christ purchased with his blood, namely, the offered promise of the Spirit.

But note well how Paul tells us this latter blessing is to be made ours; it becomes ours *by faith*. No one doubts how we receive the blessing of Abraham (righteousness, justification); all agree that it is by faith. *Therefore, having been justified by faith, we have peace with God through our Lord Jesus Christ* (Romans 5:1). But how blind we are to see, how slow to take it in – in spite of the plain declarations of Scripture – that *the promise of the Spirit* is similarly received by faith!

The Holy Spirit is the gift of the Father and of the Son (Luke 11:13). This gift is received by faith. This is the whole matter in a nutshell. Of all the sublime things in God's sublime Book, there is surely not anything more sublime than this: that a cleansed and consecrated believer may claim and receive the fullness of the Spirit by simple faith here and now. It is the greatest gift that even the exalted Christ has in his power to bestow upon his people. *Be filled with the Spirit,* says the Holy Spirit. Note that the command is in the passive voice, *be filled*; that is, let yourself be filled.

The fullness is pressing in upon you; only let it in! Receive it, and it is yours! Do you have it? If not, deal with the Lord about it at once, in a similar manner to this: "Lord Jesus, you command me to be filled with the Spirit. I take your command and make it my prayer, 'Lord, fill me with your Spirit.' You have told me *that all things for which you pray and ask, believe that you have received them, and they will be granted you* (Mark 11:24). It is your desire to fill me; it is my desire to be filled. I have made 'Lord, fill me' the prayer of my heart. I claim the fullness. I believe for it. I receive it now by faith. I have received it. I have it. It is mine. Lord, I thank you for filling me, even me, with your Holy Spirit."

And the blessed business is done! It is yours to believe, to receive. It is his to fill. Go on your way now, believing that you are filled, and God will make the belief good. It is your responsibility to keep believing. It is God's to keep you filled. Do not stagger at the promise of God through unbelief, but be made strong in faith, giving glory to God. Some object to this quick, almost instantaneous, and easy way of receiving this greatest of the New Testament blessings. But every objection urged against receiving the fullness of the Spirit in this way applies with equal, if not greater, force to a sinner who receives the pardon of his sins when he comes to God at first.

It is always in grace that God deals with sinners and justifies them the instant they believe in Jesus. It is always in grace that God deals with the justified ones and fills them with the Holy Spirit the moment they receive the fullness by faith. Eternal life is the gift of God, and all the sinner has to do is to take it. The Holy Spirit is a gift, and all God's child has to do is to take it.

But some will still object and say that it is necessary to spend some time waiting on God for the fullness before we can get it. They say a night of prayer, or a half night at least, a more or less prolonged season must be spent before we can hope to receive the blessing we desire. Of course, not one word can be uttered against spending seasons of prayer by day or by night in waiting upon God. We have the example of the Man of prayer himself before us in this. But this much must be said, that many a person has spent whole days and nights and weeks in earnest crying to God for the infilling of the Holy Spirit, and all in vain. All in vain? Why? How? Because of unbelief.

If you want to fill a corked bottle with water, and you take it to a running tap but neglect to remove the cork, how long will you have to wait holding it under the tap before it is filled? Remove the cork, and the bottle is running over in a few seconds! Many a person has cried and waited, and waited and cried for the fullness of the Spirit, but the stopper of unbelief has been in their empty hearts, and so no wonder they did not get what they wanted! Of what use will all God's giving be if a person does not receive? God cannot give and receive too!

A Christian man came to me once expecting a word of encouragement and approval and said, "I have been seeking that blessing for over thirty years."

"Brother, it's nearly time you got it then!" was the swift response.

For all these years during which the man was crying, "Give, give, give!" God was saying, "Take, take, take! Receive, receive, for I do give!"

If I heard my little girl of three years old crying piteously for a piece of bread, knowing that she must be very hungry and that I have the bread by me, would I tell her to cry on for another hour and then I might attend to her wants?

How much more – oh, how much more – will your heavenly Father give the Holy Spirit to those who ask him! But what if, in spite of her crying and of my offering, my daughter would not take the bread I offered, but still went on with her crying, "Father, oh father, do give me a piece of bread. I am so hungry!"

You silly child! Oh, how many silly children the Father has in his family, crying year in and year out, "Give, give!" and the Father yearns over them all the while saying, "Take, take, my child!"

Let some of us stop crying and set to work receiving. Take and thank! Receive and thank! *That we might receive the promise of the Spirit through faith* (Galatians 3:14).

Chapter 13

How the Filling Comes

How does the filling of the Spirit come? Does it come once for all, or is it always coming? This is what a young candidate for the baptism of the Holy Spirit once asked me. There are many asking the same questions. We have considered how the fullness is obtained, but now we proceed to consider, how does the fullness come?

In speaking of the blessing of being filled with the Spirit, the New Testament writers use three tenses in the Greek – the aorist, the imperfect, and the present. Each of these tenses has a different shade of meaning. The inspiring Spirit has employed these different tenses for a purpose, and it will be to our benefit to try and get at that purpose, to note the differences, and to learn his meaning.

The aorist tense: this is a tense to which the English

language is a stranger – it generally denotes a sudden, definite act of the past, something done and finished with. An example is, "they were filled," as in Acts 2:4: *And they were all filled with the Holy Spirit and began to speak with other tongues, as the Spirit was giving them utterance.*

The imperfect tense: this denotes, as in English, a past progressive tense. It is an action that is ongoing with no defined beginning or end. An example is a verb in the Greek that would indicate they were being filled (literally), as in Acts 13:52: *And the disciples were continually filled with joy and with the Holy Spirit.*

The present tense: this one also denotes, as in English, what its name implies. An example demonstrates "full" as the normal condition, as in Acts 11:24: *For he was a good man, and full of the Holy Spirit and of faith. And considerable numbers were brought to the Lord.*

Next we will look at passages in Acts in which the various tenses are found.

Examples of the Aorist Tense

It filled the whole house (Acts 2:2). *They were all filled with the Holy Spirit* (Acts 2:4). Peter was already filled at this time and he was there. *Then Peter, filled with the Holy Spirit* (Acts 4:8).

And they were all filled with the Holy Spirit (Acts 4:31). Peter was again among them.

Peter received a filling in the aorist tense in Acts 2:4, again in 4:8, and yet again in 4:31. So an aorist filling may be repeated and repeated again and yet again. On both occasions – in 4:8 and 4:31 – there was special need, and to meet this special need, Peter received a fresh and special and definite filling of the Holy Spirit.

From this we learn that to equip us for every new, important or difficult service to which we may be called, the Lord Jesus is prepared to grant us a fresh infilling, a refilling of the Holy Spirit. These refillings may be, and ought to be, repeated just as often as the need arises. We see it reported twice in one chapter that Peter was refilled. It will be noted that for the reasons already mentioned in chapter 8 of this book, the expression "a fresh infilling of the Holy Spirit," or refilling, is used instead of "received a fresh baptism of the Holy Spirit."

We see in Acts 9:17 referring to Saul, *And be filled with the Holy Spirit.* Saul was not to begin his life work until he was baptized – *filled with the Holy Spirit.* He must receive the very same blessing and equipment as the other apostles received at Pentecost. This was Saul's Pentecost, and for him – as for others – service began at Pentecost.

We read, *But Saul, who was also known as Paul, filled with the Holy Spirit* (Acts 13:9). The man who was filled in chapter 9 of Acts is filled anew in this passage. The aorist blessing is repeated, equipping him for the special work on hand, namely, administering that scathing rebuke to Elymas the sorcerer. In all these passages, the blessing is spoken of as a crisis (a moment), not as a process.

Examples of the Imperfect Tense

And the disciples were continually filled with joy and with the Holy Spirit (Acts 13:52). This is the only passage in Acts where the imperfect tense is used. It is not the aorist tense, "were filled," but the imperfect – "were being filled" – implying the inflow, not only to make up for, but also to sustain, the outflow.

The same idea of the imperfect is seen in Ephesians 5:18, *be filled with the Spirit*, where Principal Moule, whom I mentioned in chapter 10, points out that the Greek verb rendered "be filled" may be rendered with equal correctness as "be filling with the Holy Spirit." The preceptive verb is in the present or continuing tense and it commands a course, a habit, so that in this sense the fullness is always coming; it is spoken of as a process, not as a crisis (moment).

Examples of the Present Tense

Acts 6:3 says, *Therefore, brethren, select from among you seven men of good reputation, full of the Spirit and of wisdom, whom we may put in charge of this task* – men whose normal condition was full of the Holy Spirit. It is well worth noticing the business for which these deacons were wanted; they were to look after temporal affairs, to feed a few decent, old, Greek widows, and yet even for this business the men must be full of the Holy Spirit! None other need apply.

How far the church of today has strayed from apostolic practice! When an election of office-bearers takes place nowadays for men to manage something like the temporal affairs of Christ's church, whoever thinks of looking out for men *full of the Holy Spirit*? Many a man is elected to office in the church of the living God who does not have the Spirit of Christ at all – who is therefore not a child of God, much less full of the Holy Spirit.

"He is a man of social position, a man of means, and if he is not full of the Holy Spirit, he is at least full of this world's goods, and you know he will be a pillar in our church," someone might say. Yes, as someone has well remarked, he will be a "cater-pillar!" The church of the New Testament does not need pillars of that kind. The church of Jesus Christ and his apostles does not need to be propped up by children of the devil. What right do we have to ask an "alien," a man who is without Christ, *having no hope, and without God in the world* (Ephesians 2:12), to assist in managing and controlling our Father's house? Such was not apostolic practice.

Do not be bound together with unbelievers (2 Corinthians 6:14). There is such a great amount of unequal yoking in many of our churches, although the church's Lord expressly forbids it! *You shall not plow with an ox and a donkey together* (Deuteronomy 22:10).

Who is responsible for this unequal yoking? Isn't it the church members who elect these men and put them into office in the church of God? Church members, beware the next time offices are to be filled in your church, whether they have to do with the temporal affairs or with the spiritual, and remember apostolic advice: *Seek out among you . . . men . . . full of the Holy Spirit and wisdom.* When we get back to apostolic practice in this matter, we may hope to get back apostolic blessing, but not until then.

In Acts 6:5 we read of *Stephen, a man full of faith and of the Holy Spirit.* In those brave days of the past it was a case of demand and supply. Wanted: seven men full of the Holy Spirit. And immediately they were available! Is the trouble nowadays in the demand or in the supply? It's in both. The demand for Spirit-filled men is very lacking, but even if the demand revived tomorrow, how deplorably few could be found in our churches who bear the trademark as "up to sample"!

Still, signs of revival in both demand and supply are not lacking. Let's remember that Stephen's companions were men full of the Holy Spirit, although Stephen is the only one of whom it is expressly stated. He was the most remarkable man of the seven, a man in whom the graces of the Spirit shone with obvious brightness. His faith was so mighty that special mention needs to be made of it. It is not sufficient to describe him as a man full of the Holy Spirit, but it must be stated that he was a man full of faith *and* of the Holy Spirit. Faith was his outstanding grace.

Being full of the Holy Spirit, he (Acts 7:55). This was Stephen's normal condition right up to the very end of his life; it was true of him when we get our first glimpse of him, and it was true also as he passes through the veil into the unspeakable glory.

Barnabas *was a good man and full of the Holy Spirit* (Acts 11:24). A good man indeed, and so full of the Spirit of God that there was no room for self, for we read that he came into the midst of a great revival – a revival of which he had no hand in bringing about – and instead of being filled with envy at the divinely chosen instruments, instead of picking holes in the work and depreciating the whole movement, he was filled with gladness. We read that he *rejoiced* (Acts 11:23).

It is obvious this man was *full of the Holy Spirit.* How many there are nowadays who are not like Barnabas!

* * *

Having now considered the passages in which the various tenses are used, we are able to answer the question: How does the blessing come? Does it come once for all, or is it always coming? There are sudden, definite fillings repeated with more or less frequency, times when the believer is conscious of being filled, and when he can say, "I was filled." Between this experience – "filled" (which is an aorist blessing) – and that which should be the normal experience of every Christian, meaning "full" (which is a present blessing), it is evident that there is a great gap. But God has graciously bridged the gap for us; the connecting link between the aorist (were filled) and the present (full) is the imperfect (were being filled), so that the blessing is always coming.

Does it come once for all? A thousand times, no! If by once for all it is meant that we are reservoirs into which the fullness is poured so that once we are filled, we are independent of fresh supplies from the Lord Jesus, that surely would be a curse instead of a blessing! What reservoir is there that does not need replenishing?

Some Christians say that at times after some piece of service has been finished, they feel as if they were empty, as if their souls had been quite drained and now they are dry and thirsty. It doesn't need to be this way. It is not this way with the Spirit-filled worker whose faith is in active exercise, for he is being filled all the time.

Filled from the Reservoir

In traveling between Melbourne and my home I often stop at a wayside trough to give the horse a drink. I notice the trough is quite full of water and there is a box in one end of it. After the horse drinks, the water lowers, and soon I hear a sound as of a running tap. Yes, the sound comes from the box. That box covers a mechanism that needs explaining. Within it there is a tap connected by pipes with the Yan Yean Reservoir up in the Plenty Ranges. A metal ball is attached by a lever to the tap, which rests on the surface of the water. As the horse drinks, the water on which the ball floats is lowered, and thus the ball is lowered; the lowering of the ball opens the tap and the Yan Yean begins to pour in, so that, although the water is withdrawn by the thirsty animal, a fresh supply is poured in and the trough is being filled so that it is always full.

May it be this way with the soul of the believer. No matter what the outflow into the surrounding emptiness may be, or the withdrawals by thirsty, needy souls, there is the continual inflow, so that there may be the constant fullness. Indeed, the outflow depends directly on the inflow; one can only give as he gets. It is our responsibility to see to the connection between us and the infinite reservoir way up among the hills of God that is kept open. It is up to us to see that the tap is kept in proper working order by faith and prayer and meditation, and then, one might almost say the heart will be kept full automatically, filled with all the fullness of God, no matter what the spiritual drain upon us may be. For now it is not a question of our capacity to contain, but a question of God's infinite supply for all our needs.

This is also the explanation of the overflow, the flowing rivers of John 7:38. It's the overflow, and only the overflow, that blesses. There is not a drop for thirsty souls until someone overflows. It is the overflow in the Sunday school class and in the pulpit, and for that matter, in every other sphere of Christian service that brings blessing; this overflow is in direct proportion to the inflow. Rivers cannot flow out unless rivers first flow in.

An ordinary service pipe in our domestic water supply may serve to illustrate some of the points we have been considering. We take a bucket to the tap for water, and suddenly there is none. Something is wrong. Either the authorities have cut off our supply because of some infraction of the law on our part, or there is an obstruction in our service pipe, or the pressure is insufficient to give us even a drop, or the supply is so deficient that it has been shut off from us for a time so it may be sent in another direction. Unfortunately, sometimes the flow of the living waters from the soul of the believer ceases; but the ordinary round of duty, either in the community visiting, or in the Sunday school class, or in the pulpit has not ceased; a ceaseless stream of talk may still flow on, but there is no living water in it at all.

Why? It is not that the pressure behind us – the pressure in the infinite reservoir way up among the hills of God – is insufficient or that the supply is deficient, unable to meet our needs because it is supplying needy ones elsewhere. God's water supply never breaks down or fails, as we often experience with our city supply. If the flowing has ceased, it is for one of two reasons: either God has, in mercy and in judgment, cut off the supply, or there is an obstruction in us, and sin is at the bottom of both reasons.

> *Search me, O God, and know my heart;*
> *Try me and know my anxious thoughts;*
> *And see if there be any hurtful way in*
> *me, And lead me in the everlasting way.*
> (Psalm 139:23-24)

Confession and cleansing is the divinely appointed method for making right what has gone wrong.

Sometimes on going to the tap we find there is water, but it is such a miserable dribble! It might be from insufficient pressure or some partial obstruction in the pipe, or perhaps it is because we have not opened the tap fully. What a wretched parody we see between the flowing rivers of John 7:38 and the life and service of many of the Christians of today!

Some of the living water no doubt comes from them, but it only percolates through, dribbling and trickling out of them. Why? Certainly not from insufficient pressure, as has been already remarked; the fault and the failure is not on God's side. But there is some local obstruction – amounting in many a case to almost entire obstruction – some little idol or other in our heart, if not a sin, yet certainly a weight (Hebrews 12:1), and this hinders the outflow. Confession and cleansing are still God's remedy.

The hindrance may be our unbelief, which limits *the Holy One of Israel* (Psalm 78:41) and opens the tap only a little instead of opening it fully. This is when we expect little when we were divinely authorized to expect much. It happens when we refuse to obey the command, *Open thy mouth wide, and I will fill it* (Psalm 81:10). Rivers cannot flow through a heart full of unbelief.

Sometimes, again, we go to the tap and get a little

water and a great deal of air. What a noise! Air is a very good thing in its own place, but that is not in a water pipe; that is meant to convey water and nothing else, and for the water pipe to do its work, it is necessary that it be emptied and cleansed of everything else, even of air. Scripture has said that some things puff up, and there is a good deal of "puff" in some hearts through which the living water is supposed to be flowing. God be merciful to us! Such hearts, like our water pipe, need emptying and cleansing.

Yet once more, on going to the tap, we find a splendid supply; the pipe is clean, the pressure is good. Before we open the tap, the pipe is full of water. When the tap is opened and the bucket fills, the pipe is still full, for although the water pours out at the tap, it pours in at the reservoir so that the pipe is kept full, even though the tap is open and the water streams from it.

When the tap is shut, you cannot say any more about the pipe now, other than that it is still full of water. May it be this way with the believer who is spiritually adjusted. When resting at his Master's feet he is full; when actively engaged in service he is still full; his normal condition is *full of the Holy Spirit* because he has learned how to obey the command, *be filled with the Spirit* (Ephesians 5:18).

Chapter 14

The Effects of Fullness

Among the effects and benefits that accompany and flow from being filled with the Holy Spirit in this life, we see the following qualities emerge.

Courage

"Oh, I could not do that. I do not have the courage," is a reply frequently made by Christian people when asked to undertake some type of service or other for the Master. The first point to be settled is, "Is that the Master's will for me?" If so, lack of courage is a confession to the lack of the fullness of the Holy Spirit. The Spirit-filled man knows the fear of God and knows no other fear.

Let's look at Peter's example. *But Peter, taking his stand with the eleven, raised his voice and declared to them* (Acts 2:14). There is no fear of servant maids now like he had in the courtyard! But can this be the man who cowered when *a servant-girl came to him and said, "You too were with Jesus the Galilean"* (Matthew 26:69)? Can this be the man who *began to curse and swear, "I do not know the man!"* (v. 74)?

The very same, and yet not the same, for the baptism of the Holy Spirit has changed Peter the cowardly hearted into Peter the lionhearted so that he can stand before that surging multitude, their hands dyed crimson in his Master's blood, and without a tremor he can charge them with the awful crime: *You nailed to a cross by the hands of godless men and put Him to death* (Acts 2:23).

> *Now as they observed the confidence of Peter and John and understood that they were uneducated and untrained men, they were amazed, and began to recognize them as having been with Jesus.* (Acts 4:13)
>
> *And when they had prayed, the place where they had gathered together was shaken, and they were all filled with the Holy Spirit and began to speak the word of God with boldness.* (Acts 4:31)

Acts 5:20 says, *Go, stand and speak to the people in the*

temple the whole message of this Life. They were taken out of prison and ordered to go and do again the very thing for which they had been imprisoned! But they were Spirit-filled men, and so we read in the next verse, *they entered into the temple.* A few verses later we read, *But Peter and the apostles answered, "We must obey God rather than men"* (Acts 5:29). They were beaten (v. 40), but their response to the persecution was:

> *So they went on their way from the presence of the Council, rejoicing that they had been considered worthy to suffer shame for His name. And every day, in the temple and from house to house, they kept right on teaching and preaching Jesus as the Christ.* (Acts 5:41-42)

Paul said, *For I am ready not only to be bound, but even to die at Jerusalem for the name of the Lord Jesus* (Acts 21:13). The apostles were courage-filled because they were Spirit-filled!

The Fruit of the Spirit

The fruit of the Spirit will be manifest in the life of someone who is filled with the Holy Spirit. This includes love, joy, peace, etc. (Galatians 5:22-23). How can one's life be filled with the fruit of the Spirit unless one's heart is first filled with the Spirit himself? In the primitive church, the men and women were filled with the Holy Spirit; that was the rule. Now, sadly, it has come to be the exception, but as a consequence we see how in the primitive church their lives were enriched by the fruit of the Spirit.

Love: *And the congregation of those who believed were of one heart and soul; and not one of them claimed that anything belonging to him was his own, but all things were common property to them* (Acts 4:32). This may be poor political economy, but it is good spiritual economy, a simple Bible illustration of the Bible instruction, *store up for yourselves treasures in heaven* (Matthew 6:20). If brotherly love was spread around today, how soon the present trouble would disappear! As the best available commentary on this heavenly word *love*, study all of 1 Corinthians 13 on your knees.

Joy: *They were taking their meals together with gladness and sincerity of heart, praising God* (Acts 2:46-47). Every meal was a sacrament. The same cause would produce the same result today.

So they went on their way from the presence of the Council, rejoicing that they had been considered worthy to suffer shame for His name (Acts 5:41), when some of us would have been bemoaning ourselves and complaining about the hardness of our situation!

When the Jews *and the devout women of promi-nence and the leading men of the city . . . instigated a persecution against Paul and Barnabas,* Paul and Barnabas *shook off the dust of their feet . . . And the disciples were continually filled with joy and with the Holy Spirit* (Acts 13:50-52).

In prison, *Paul and Silas were praying and singing hymns of praise to God* (Acts 16:25). The heavier the tribulation, the more their joy seemed to overflow. Paul wrote, *I am overflowing with joy in all our affliction* (2 Corinthians 7:4). And of course, the heavier the tribu-lation, the more joy they needed to sustain them. *For the joy of the LORD is your strength* (Nehemiah 8:10).

Peace: When Stephen appeared before the council on false charges, the council *saw his face like the face of an angel* (Acts 6:15). Later, when they stoned Stephen, he called *on the Lord and said, "Lord Jesus, receive my spirit!" Then falling on his knees, he cried out with a loud voice, "Lord, do not hold this sin against them!" Having said this, he fell asleep* (Acts 7:59-60).

Paul wrote, *We are afflicted in every way, but not crushed; perplexed, but not despairing; persecuted, but not forsaken; struck down, but not destroyed* (2 Corinthians 4:8-9).

Thus we might go through the heavenly list – long-suffering, gentleness, goodness, faith, meekness, temperance – and see how richly the fruit flourished in the lives of those in Bible times who were Spirit-filled.

Before moving forward let's notice where it is that joy grows. It grows between love and peace. It is, as someone has well called it, a sheltered fruit. If love withers, joy is exposed on that side, and it too will fade. If peace is interfered with, even though love is vigorous, joy is exposed on that side now, and it will fade away and die. The only way to preserve joy in vigorous growth is to see that its sheltering fruits, love and peace, are kept free from blight and remain vigorous too.

In his letter to the Ephesian church, to whom he addressed the command, *Be filled with the Spirit*, Paul points out very clearly what the results of the fullness will be:

1) A singing heart (Ephesians 5:19). This is what would bring us and our lives up to concert pitch. We would not go "flat" anymore. This would drive away the leaden dullness.

2) A thankful heart (v. 20). Such a heart would not find fault with Christ's government, will find *no cause for stumbling in* Jesus (1 John 2:10), and will not be offended at him (Matthew 11:6) no matter how he may test and try it. *Blessed is he* that has such a heart in his chest!

3) A submissive heart (v. 21). *With humility of mind regard one another as more important than yourselves*

(Philippians 2:3). The things that were once impossible will be possible.

4) Spirit-filled wives will be in submission to their own husbands (Ephesians 5:22).

5) Spirit-filled husbands will love their wives as Christ loved the church (v. 25).

6) Spirit-filled children will obey their parents (Ephesians 6:1).

7) Spirit-filled fathers will not provoke their children to wrath (v. 4).

8) Spirit-filled servants (bondslaves) will be obedient to their masters (v. 5).

9) Spirit-filled masters will treat their servants as they (the masters) would wish to be treated by their Master (v. 9).

Wouldn't results 8 and 9 above be the best possible solution of the constantly recurring labor and capital difficulty, and render a labor war impossible because it would be unnecessary?

10) Spirit-filled men will be strong in the Lord – spiritual giants and not sickly, hunchbacked spiritual dwarfs (v. 10).

11) Spirit-filled men will be warriors, clad in the whole armor of God; if not Spirit-filled they could not carry it (v. 11).

12) Spirit-filled soldiers will not war against flesh and blood; internal foes will have all been subdued,

the civil war having ceased; their enemies would now be external, and they would be free to concentrate all their attention and God-inspired energies on them. Their enemies are first in the world – principalities and world rulers, and second in the heavenlies – powers and spiritual hosts of wickedness (v. 12).

13) Spirit-filled men will be always praying in the Spirit (v. 18). In order to have this vigilance, watching is also needed.

Such are some of the results on the positive side of being filled with the Spirit. The effects on the negative side are manifest in Galatians 5:16-17. *But I say, walk by the Spirit, and you will not carry out the desire of the flesh. For the flesh sets its desire against the Spirit, and the Spirit against the flesh; for these are in opposition to one another, so that you [walking by the Spirit] may not do the things that you please [if you were walking by the flesh].* See Galatians 5:19-21 for the list of examples of walking in the flesh.

Reaching the Masses

Another effect of a Spirit-baptized church would be that the masses would be reached. See how the early church – which was a Spirit-baptized church and persistently kept that truth in the foreground – reached the masses, and what blessed results they saw! They were not amused or entertained, but they were converted, saved, and turned to the Lord.

> *And that day there were added about three thousand souls.* (Acts 2:41)

> *The number of the men came to be about five thousand.* (Acts 4:4)

> *And all the more believers in the Lord, multitudes of men and women, were constantly added to their number.* (Acts 5:14)

> *The number of the disciples continued to increase greatly in Jerusalem, and a great many of the priests were becoming obedient to the faith.* (Acts 6:7)

> *The crowds [in Samaria] with one accord were giving attention to what was said by Philip.* (Acts 8:6)

> *And all who lived at Lydda and Sharon saw him, and they turned to the Lord.* (Acts 9:35)

> *It became known all over Joppa, and many believed in the Lord.* (Acts 9:42)

> *While Peter was still speaking these words,*

the Holy Spirit fell upon all those who were listening to the message. (Acts 10:44)

And the hand of the Lord was with them, and a large number who believed turned to the Lord. (Acts 11:21)

The next Sabbath nearly the whole city assembled to hear the word of the Lord. (Acts 13:44)

And spoke in such a manner that a large number of people believed, both of Jews and of Greeks. (Acts 14:1)

After they had preached the gospel to that city and had made many disciples. (Acts 14:21)

So the churches . . . were increasing in number daily. (Acts 16:5)

These men who have upset the world have come here also. (Acts 17:6)

Crispus, . . . believed in the Lord with all his household, and many of the Corinthians when they heard were believing and being baptized. (Acts 18:8)

Many also of those who had believed kept

> *coming. So the word of the Lord was grow-*
> *ing mightily and prevailing.* (Acts 19:18, 20).

We often hear of discussions on the "lapsed masses."

"Why have the masses of the people lapsed from the churches?" Perhaps the more correct way of putting it would be, why have the churches lapsed from the masses?

The answer is not hard to find, because they have lost the driving power that alone could keep them abreast of the masses, even the baptism of the Holy Spirit. The conditions were just as unfavorable in the first century as in the nineteenth century, and yet we read, *So the word of the Lord was growing mightily and prevailing.* It is positively painful to see the substitutes that people try today for the power of the Holy Spirit. They are all miserable substitutes!

One church tries this plan, another that, and not one of them has found a new plan that is a permanent success. They are floundering (struggling), and some of them are foundering (failing), and no wonder. It will be no loss to the kingdom of God if churches that ignore the Holy Spirit should founder. Let's get back to Pentecostal methods.

The trouble is that the churches have lost their way to that "upper room." Let a church find her way back there and obtain her Pentecost; let those in the pulpit and pews be baptized with the Holy Spirit, and the people will come running in. That church will not need to cater using amusements as a bait to catch the masses, but the people will come crowding into her pews, climbing into them as Zacchaeus climbed into the branches of that sycamore tree when he wanted to see the Lord; for the people still want to see Jesus, and they have heard that He is *to pass through that way* (Luke 19:4). We cannot improve on Pentecost's methods for reaching the masses.

Persecution

Yet another effect of the fullness of the Spirit must be mentioned: persecution.

> *Others were mocking and saying, "They are full of sweet wine."* (Acts 2:13)

> *They laid hands on them and put them in jail.* (Acts 4:3)

> *Let us warn them.* (Acts 4:17)

> *They laid hands on the apostles and put them in a public jail.* (Acts 5:18)

> *They were cut to the quick and intended to kill them.* (Acts 5:33)

After calling the apostles in, they flogged them and ordered them not to speak in the name of Jesus. (Acts 5:40)

And dragged him away and brought him before the Council. (Acts 6:12)

They went on stoning Stephen. (Acts 7:59)

And on that day a great persecution began against the church in Jerusalem. (Acts 8:1)

Dragging off men and women, he [Saul] would put them in prison. (Acts 8:3)

Now Saul, still breathing threats and murder against the disciples of the Lord. (Acts 9:1)

The Jews plotted together to do away with him. (Acts 9:23)

They were attempting to put him to death. (Acts 9:29)

Had James the brother of John put to death with a sword. (Acts 12:2)

He put him [Peter] in prison. (Acts 12:4)

Instigated a persecution against Paul and Barnabas. (Acts 13:50)

Embittered them against the brethren.
(Acts 14:2)

To mistreat and to stone them. (Acts 14:5)

They stoned Paul. (Acts 14:19)

*Proceeded to order them to be beaten with
rods [Paul and Silas].* (Acts 16:22)

*When they had struck them with
many blows, they threw them into
prison, . . . and fastened their feet in the
stocks.* (Acts 16:23-24)

*Formed a mob and set the city in an
uproar; and attacking the house of Jason.*
(Acts 17:5)

Agitating and stirring up the crowds.
(Acts 17:13)

They resisted and blasphemed. (Acts 18:6)

*The Jews with one accord rose up against
Paul and brought him before the judgment
seat.* (Acts 18:12)

*Speaking evil of the Way before the people,
. . . took away the disciples, reasoning daily.*
(Acts 19:9)

No small disturbance concerning the Way.
(Acts 19:23)

Filled with rage. (Acts 19:28)

A plot was formed against him by the Jews.
(Acts 20:3)

In this way the Jews at Jerusalem will bind the man who owns this belt and deliver him into the hands of the Gentiles. (Acts 21:11)

And laid hands on him. (Acts 21:27) (Paul was never free after this.)

While they were seeking to kill him.
(Acts 21:31)

Beating Paul . . . bound with two chains . . . into the barracks. (Acts 21:32-34)

He should not be allowed to live.
(Acts 22:22)

The Jews formed a conspiracy and bound themselves under an oath, saying that they would neither eat nor drink until they had killed Paul. (Acts 23:12)

They proceeded to deliver Paul and some other prisoners to a centurion. (Acts 27:1)

From now on let no one cause trouble for
me, for I bear on my body the brand-marks
of Jesus. (Galatians 6:17)

All of this makes lively reading in this peaceful, easy-going day of ours, and yet the world has changed in its attitude or feeling toward God and the things of God. But a most palpable change has taken place somewhere. The change is unfortunately in us, in the people of God, a change that is not for the better.

We have lost that which brought these men into direct collision with the world and with its ways, even the fullness of the Spirit. Let someone in our day just seek and obtain the blessing that made these men mighty for God, and they will soon find that the world has not changed and that the Pharisees have not changed either; the fullness of the Holy Spirit makes someone the uncompromising friend of God, and that certainly involves the hostility of the world. *Because of this the world hates you* (John 15:19).

It is wise for those who seek the fullness of the Spirit to remember these facts and to count the cost, for the persecution may come from the most unlikely, least looked-for places. To be forewarned is to be forearmed. *In the world you have tribulation, but take courage; I have overcome the world* (John 16:33).

Chapter 15

How Do We Know
We Are Filled?

The question is often asked: How am I to know when I am filled with the Holy Spirit? There are three ways to know it.

The Written Word

First, you may know it from the testimony of the written Word of God. *Therefore I say to you, all things for which you pray and ask, believe that you have received them, and they will be granted you* (Mark 11:24). From this you know that if you have to the best of your ability fulfilled the conditions necessary for the filling of the Holy Spirit, on praying and asking for the fullness, it is your privilege to believe that you have received what you have asked for; actually, it is your bound duty in compliance with Christ's express command to believe this.

If God gives and you really receive, you may then give thanks, and that proves that you possess it, for you cannot truly give thanks for what you do not possess! It will be noted that this answer is precisely similar to the answer that would be given to the question: How am I to know that I am saved? By simple faith on the testimony of the Word.

As multitudes have accepted salvation without any emotion, without any feeling whatsoever, so also many have accepted the fullness of the Holy Spirit by faith without any wave of emotion or feeling that bears witness to evidence of the filling. But this is not to say that there is never any feeling or that the emotions are never stirred; not so, for the feelings will come in God's own time.

Witness of the Spirit

The second way one may know that the fullness has come is the witness of the infilling Spirit. Just as in multitudes of cases, the blessed Spirit bears witness with the blood when it is applied at the moment of conversion, so many people know in their inner consciousness the moment when the fullness of the Spirit was given; they felt the incoming and can date their baptism, as others have felt the regenerating change and can date their conversion.

It should also be repeated here that as many are unaware of the date of their conversion, though well assured of the fact, likewise, many may be unaware of the date of their baptism with the Holy Spirit, though well assured that they have entered the blessed life. If we are assured that we have received the fullness of the Spirit, we do not need to worry about dates.

Signs Following

The third way someone may know whether the fullness has come to his heart and life is by the signs following, by what "The Men" of the North of Scotland would call "the marks."[23]

Christ's words used in another connection may surely be applied in this: *You will know them by their fruits* (Matthew 7:20). *But the fruit of the Spirit is love, joy, peace, patience, kindness, goodness, faithfulness, gentleness, self-control* (Galatians 5:22-23). The fullness of the fruit will surely be found where the fullness of the Spirit is. Quantity and quality will both be

---

23   It is possible that MacNeil speaks here of two footprints in the Scottish Highlands where nothing will grow. They are said to be the footprints of evangelist Finlay Munro, who, when questioned about the truth of his preaching there in 1827, said the ground where he stood would bear witness to the truth of what he said and nothing would grow in those spots.

there. As this has already been touched upon when considering the effects of the blessing, no more needs to be added here. This, however, must be clearly kept in mind: while the fullness of the Spirit is a gift, the fruit of the Spirit is growth.

Fruit grows, and the fruit will grow if only we make sure the conditions are present that are favorable to growth. That man who expects full growth without attending to the conditions of growth does not manifest much wisdom.

Chapter 16

May I Say I Am Filled?

The question has been raised: Is it right for someone to say they are filled with the Holy Spirit? Couldn't this have the taste of egotism? John said of Jesus, *Behold the Lamb of God, who takes away the sin of the world. . . . this is the One who baptizes in the Holy Spirit* (John 1:29, 33). Christ's twofold role here is to take away sin and to baptize with the Holy Spirit.

Each person who knows Christ as the sin-bearer should have an experiential acquaintance with him as the baptizer too. Certainly this alone is full salvation. To have sin taken away is only half of salvation; to be baptized with the Holy Spirit as well is to possess full salvation.

Now, if Christ has taken away a man's sin, can't that man know it? Certainly. And if he knows it, can't he bear witness to the fact? Truly, doesn't Christ expect him to confess – to tell what great things the Lord has done for him?

No right-thinking person would regard it as wrong for a saved man to confess his Savior or would regard his confession as egotism. By uniformity of reasoning, if Christ has baptized a pardoned man with the Holy Spirit, can't that man know it? Surely! And if he knows it, can't he bear witness to the fact? Couldn't he tell what still greater things the Lord has done for him? Would this be wrong? Must this necessarily be egotism?

At the same time, it is perfectly scriptural when questioned about it for a Spirit-filled man to testify for Christ's glory about the infilling of the Holy Spirit – for we must be careful not to slander the grace of God that is in us and not to grieve the Holy Spirit by ignoring him or his work within us; one cannot be too careful in case he would be found casting his *pearls before swine* (Matthew 7:6). As a rule, it will be better in this matter to let the life speak rather than the tongue. Indeed, it will not often be necessary for the Spirit-filled man to be questioned on the subject at all; his speech will betray him, as will his manner of life and his fruitful service.

Chapter 17

Does Anyone Lose the Blessing?

The question trembles from many a lip: If I get the blessing, may I lose it? Most certainly. But, glory be to God! He has made ample provision for failure. There is no reason why we should fail; God has made ample provision against failure, and we must not expect to fail. But in case we do fail, provision has been made.

The most prolific cause of loss is disobedience – disobedience either to one of God's written commands or to the inward promptings of his Holy Spirit – *the Holy Spirit, whom God has given to those who obey Him* (Acts 5:32). This all-glorious gift is not only obtained but also retained in connection with obedience. It is absolutely necessary to maintain the attitude of complete self-surrender, for the slightest act of disobedience – that is, the asserting of our own will in opposition to his will – may cost us the loss of the blessing. For example, neglecting to speak to a man about the great salvation, or refusing to give a tract to someone when we knew God wanted us to do so. We must learn to be obedient to the promptings of the Spirit. *My eyes are continually toward the LORD* (Psalm 25:15) must be our constant attitude.

If we possess the blessing and desire to retain it, there is another matter of the last importance that we must attend to – letting *the word of Christ richly dwell within you, with all wisdom* (Colossians 3:16). The Spirit-filled man will be a Word-filled man. A neglected Bible is responsible for much of the lost blessing from which many of God's children suffer today. If we would retain the blessing in its fullness and freshness, we must feed daily and feed much upon Christ as he is revealed to us in the Holy Scriptures. It is the function of the indwelling Spirit to take of the things of Christ and to show them to us (John 16:14). He does not speak from himself or of himself, but of Jesus, and so he will continually draw us to the Word, that he may have the opportunity of drawing our attention to fresh beauties in Immanuel. There is a lot of so-called reading of the Bible that is not *search[ing] the scriptures* (John 5:39), not delighting *in the law of the LORD*, not meditating on it *day and night* (Psalm 1:2), and not letting *the word of the Christ dwell in you in abundance.*

You cannot live a Spirit-filled life and be content with a shallow, meager acquaintance with the divine Word. The Spirit-filled person gives God's book its own proud place, the premier place, in all his reading. It is useful to compare the effects of being filled with the Spirit and of being filled with the Word.

> *Be filled with the Spirit, speaking to one another in psalms and hymns and spiritual songs, singing and making melody with your heart to the Lord.* (Ephesians 5:18-19)

> *Let the word of Christ richly dwell within you, with all wisdom teaching and admonishing one another with psalms and hymns and spiritual songs, singing with thankfulness in your hearts to God.* (Colossians 3:16)

Then have we unhappily, through disobedience or neglect, lost the blessing that once we possessed? Is there someone saying, "Oh, that I were as in months past" (Job 29:2)? It may be "all joy" with you again, for if you have lost the blessing, just go back and search for it, and you will find it where you lost it! Right there and nowhere else.

Have you found the spot where your obedience failed? Yield and obey right there, pick up your obedience where you dropped it, and there you may obtain the blessing again as you obtained it at first – but right there and nowhere else. An illustration of this is found in 2 Kings 6. The divinity students of those days were going down to build a new divinity hall on the banks of the Jordan, and they asked Elisha, the man of God, to go with them. The story tells us that as one of the students *was felling a beam, the axe head fell into the water; and he cried out and said, "Alas, my master! For it was borrowed." Then the man of God said, "Where did it fall?" And when he showed him the place, he cut off a stick and threw it in there, and made the iron float. He said, "Take it up for yourself." So he put out his hand and took it* (2 Kings 6:5-7).

Having re-fixed the axe-head on the handle, he went on again with cutting down the tree. Where was it that the student got his lost axe-head? Where he lost it! It was in the very spot where it fell into the Jordan's waters – it was right there that he found it. So if you lose the blessing, the only spot on earth where you need to look for it, if you wish to take it up again, is the very spot where you lost it.

Let's all learn by heart what the student did not do. After the axe-head flew from the handle, he did not continue at work chopping with an axe handle. No. Instead, as soon as he lost his axe-head, he stopped until he got it on again. Oh, that many a Christian worker would read, mark, learn, and inwardly digest! Then on some Sabbaths there might be many a pulpit without a preacher, many a Sunday school class without a teacher, and many a sphere of Christian labor without its worker. Why? Where are they? Away looking for their axe-heads! Away to the banks of that river of disobedience, in whose sluggish waters they lost them!

How sad that there are so many today with an axe handle who try in this way to fell beams for the house of our God! They work with the blessing lost! This is hard labor and there is very little to show for it, except earnestness! And isn't it a fine thing to be in earnest? Yes, but it is finer to have a little of that uncommon thing – ordinary common sense behind the earnestness, and the man who hews with an axe handle doesn't impress anyone as being overburdened that way!

If we have enjoyed and have lost the fullness of the Spirit, let's confess, take ourselves to the open fountain, and obey, and he will put away our sin. Then, let's start fresh, let's come to him again for the fullness as we did at the first, and we will find *yet He remains faithful, for He cannot deny Himself* (2 Timothy 2:13). For the sake of the sacred heart, for his name's glory, for the sake of souls and for our own sake, we must not and we will not try to live and labor without being *filled with the Spirit.*

Biography of John MacNeil

John MacNeil was born in Scotland in 1854 and was raised in the Central Highlands of Victoria, Australia. He was educated at Ballarat College and Melbourne University, earning a B.A. in 1874. He studied theology at New College, Edinburgh, and was ordained in 1879. MacNeil was a Presbyterian evangelist and minister, and in 1881 he began touring Australia as an itinerant preacher. Health problems forced him to take some time off the circuit shortly after he started, but he was able to eventually return again to his passion for preaching after a minister laid hands on him to pray for healing.

MacNeil's introduction to The Higher Life movement, also known as the Keswick movement, which was devoted to Christian holiness, was significant for him. He cooperated with a Methodist colleague in an evangelistic mission in Jamestown, which led to his sensing the call to evangelistic ministry.

In 1890 MacNeil and several others formed a group that came to be known as The Band, which met regularly to pray for revival. The group also focused on the need to be filled with the Holy Spirit and on being baptized in the Spirit. The Band decided to hold a Keswick-like convention in Geelong with George Grubb as the keynote speaker; he had addressed other Keswick conventions in England.

John MacNeil preached in the streets of mining towns, rode a bicycle on dusty roads to bring the gospel to mining camps and workers in tents, and preached in churches all over Australia. He delivered tracts to some and sermons to others. Wherever he went, he preached.

MacNeil married Hannah Thomas in 1884, and they had five children. But their marriage was a short one, as MacNeil collapsed suddenly and died at the age of forty-two while on tour in Queensland in 1896. His wife, Hannah, wrote his biography, *John MacNeil: Late Evangelist in Australia*, in 1897. She hand-delivered her manuscript of the biography to H. B. Macartney, who served as the editor of the book and wrote a note to the readers in the beginning of the book. According to Duncan S. McEachran in the introduction to the biography, there was nothing novel about MacNeil's preaching. It was prayer that made the difference.

Throughout the biography, Hannah MacNeil shared John's story, his journeys as a preacher, his heart as a minister, and his journals and letters. She closed the book with a letter from The Band, which was written to her after his death. In this letter they said, "We desire nothing more earnestly than to drink more deeply, as Mr. MacNeil used to drink, from the fountain of Zion's waters; to follow the Master more fully, as he used to follow with cheerful, unfaltering step; to breathe, as he used to breathe, only, always, and altogether for his King; to die as he died, in the very thick of battle; and to shine as he shall shine, like stars forever and ever."

Two collections of MacNeil's sermons, "Some One is Coming" and "Honey Gathered and Stored," were also published posthumously. Thousands of people heard the gospel and responded as a result of MacNeil's obedience to the call to ministry.

Similar Updated Classics

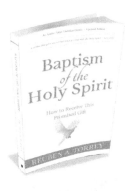

Baptism of the Holy Spirit,
by Reuben A. Torrey

Today, few people know exactly what the Scriptures say regarding the Holy Spirit, and the consequence is men trying to do things in their own strength. Sadder still is how one group denies the power of the Holy Spirit, while another group pursues the things of the Spirit more than they pursue Christ Himself. Somewhere in the middle is the truth. This book takes a close look at Scripture to see what the Lord Himself tells us regarding His Holy Spirit and how it relates to us today.

Available where books are sold.

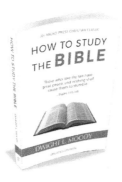

How to Study the Bible,
by Dwight L. Moody

There is no situation in life for which you cannot find some word of consolation in Scripture. If you are in affliction, if you are in adversity and trial, there is a promise for you. In joy and sorrow, in health and in sickness, in poverty and in riches, in every condition of life, God has a promise stored up in His Word for you.

Available where books are sold.

The Overcoming Life, by Dwight L. Moody

Are you an overcomer? Or, are you plagued by little sins that easily beset you? Even worse, are you failing in your Christian walk, but refuse to admit and address it? No Christian can afford to dismiss the call to be an overcomer. The earthly cost is minor; the eternal reward is beyond measure.

Available where books are sold.

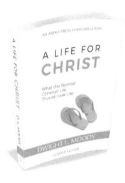

A Life for Christ, by Dwight L. Moody

In the church today, we have everything buttoned up perfectly. The music is flawless, the sermon well-prepared and smoothly delivered, and the grounds meticulously kept. People come on time and go home on time. But a fundamental element is missing. The business of church has undermined the individual's need to truly live for Christ, so much so, that only a limited few are seeing their life impact the world.

Dwight L. Moody takes us deep into Scripture and paints a clear picture of what ought to be an individual's life for Christ. The call for each Christian is to become an active member in the body of Christ. The motive is love for the Lord and our neighbor. The result will be the salvation of men, women, and children everywhere.

Available where books are sold.

The Ten Commandments,
by Dwight L. Moody

The ten commandments are not popular today. Atheists want them nowhere in sight. Many Christians say they are outdated. But Dwight L. Moody challenges us to take a closer look. Which of the ten commandments can we honestly say are not good? Which of the ten commandments can we break and not suffer the consequences, both here and in eternity?

This book will challenge you to examine God's rules for life. God doesn't ask anything of us that is difficult or unreasonable, and this is certainly true with Jesus Christ as our strength and the Holy Spirit to guide us. This book is a challenging yet refreshing look at some of the oldest, most well-known words of God.

Available where books are sold.

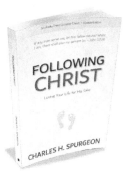

Following Christ, by Charles H. Spurgeon

You cannot have Christ if you will not serve Him. If you take Christ, you must take Him in all His qualities. You must not simply take Him as a Friend, but you must also take Him as your Master. If you are to become His disciple, you must also become His servant. God-forbid that anyone fights against that truth. It is certainly one of our greatest delights on earth to serve our Lord, and this is to be our joyful vocation even in heaven itself: *His servants shall serve Him: and they shall see His face* (Revelation 22:3-4).

Available where books are sold.

Faithful to Christ, by Charles H. Spurgeon

If there is a true faith, there must be a declaration of it. If you are a candle, and God has lit you, then *let your light so shine before men that they may see your good works and glorify your Father who is in the heavens* (Matthew 5:16). Soldiers of Christ must, like soldiers of our nation, wear their uniforms; and if they are ashamed of their uniforms, they ought to be drummed out of the army.

Available where books are sold.

How to Pray, by Reuben A. Torrey

May God use this book to inspire many who are currently prayerless, or nearly so, to pray earnestly. May God stir up your own heart to be one of those burdened to pray, and to pray until God answers.

Available where books are sold.

Pilgrim's Progress, by John Bunyan

Often disguised as something that would help him, evil accompanies Christian on his journey to the Celestial City. As you walk with him, you'll begin to identify today's many religious pitfalls. These are presented by men such as Pliable, who turns back at the Slough of Despond; and Ignorance, who believes he's a true follower of Christ when he's really only trusting in himself. Each character represented in this allegory is intentionally and profoundly accurate in its depiction of what we see all around us, and unfortunately, what we too often see in ourselves. But while Christian is injured and nearly killed, he eventually prevails to the end. So can you.

Available where books are sold.

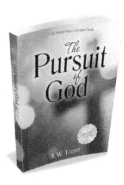

The Pursuit of God, by A.W. Tozer

Come near to the holy men and women of the past and you will soon feel the heat of their desire after God. Let A. W. Tozer's pursuit of God spur you also into a genuine hunger and thirst to truly know God.

Available where books are sold.

Made in United States
North Haven, CT
03 March 2023

33445819R00095